PRAISE FOR
READY FOR ANYTHING

A book of practical wisdom. This is my new manual for living kind, because doing life together means preparing to help others with the big stuff *and* the small stuff too. It just makes sense because there is no greater joy than being ready to help others when they need it.

> **Susy Flory,** *New York Times* bestselling
> author and coauthor, director of
> West Coast Christian Writers

Fear that the worst might happen tends to sit silently in the backs of our minds. What if a natural disaster happens, our house burns down, or even the unthinkable occurrs? What would we do? How would we protect ourselves and our families? *Ready for Anything* helps alleviate those fears by teaching us how to wisely prepare for even the most unexpected of events. Kathi's tips and advice will help you feel at peace and fully prepared for anything that might happen in the future.

> **Tracie Miles,** Proverbs 31 speaker
> and bestselling author

Kathi Lipp delivers humorous, clever, practical advice for taking stock of your pantry and your life. With pithy, authentic wit and wisdom, Lipp helps prepare you for all those unexpected bumps in the road with simple steps and action plans designed for today's busy life.

> **KariAnne Wood,** Thistlewood Farms

When the emergency worker informed us of our daughter's severe accident, adrenaline and anxiety kicked in. I couldn't think of what to pack for the drive to get by her side as soon as possible. Now I have Kathi's plan, giving me and my loved ones the confidence that if something scary happens, we have a plan.

Lynn Cowell, member of the Proverbs 31 Ministries speaking and writing team, author of *Make Your Move*

Kathi Lipp is a wise guide when wading into the waters of prepping for any crisis, large or small. *Ready for Anything* provides actionable steps that anyone can do, including those who feel the most unprepared. I grew up in a religious environment that fostered fear regarding apocalyptic disasters, but Kathi's words calmed my heart without triggering me. Since reading this book, I have already completed several steps and am more prepared today than I was when I started. "Be kind to your future self," as Kathi says, and read this book.

Anna LeBaron, author of *The Polygamist's Daughter*

I'm sorry to say, but I have not been ready for anything. Living in hurricane territory has meant I scramble, hunt, and shop at least once a year here in North Carolina. I'm thrilled to be working through Kathi Lipp's practical, doable plan so that my household will be prepared for the wind and rain this year (or any other emergency that comes our way). Kathi's strategy to include our neighbors in our prep makes me especially excited to get started!

Amy Carroll, Proverbs 31 Ministries speaker and writer, author of *Breaking Up with Perfect* and *Exhale*

Oh, let Kathi teach you how to be ready for anything! You will laugh out loud as Kathi eases you into the conversation of being prepared. She teaches you what to know and how to get started. Being prepared doesn't mean you don't trust God; it means having the resources to face emergencies or disasters when they come. Thanks, Kathi!

Wendy Pope, president of Word Up Ministries,
author of *Hidden Potential*

Recently, I received a phone call that had me rushing to get on a plane in less than thirty minutes. I was so frazzled from this unexpected family crisis that I couldn't even think of what to put in my carry-on bag. That later led to a $300 Target trip to provide what I needed for an unplanned week on the other side of the country. I wish I would have read *Ready for Anything* before this so that Kathi's wisdom could have prepared me practically for what was coming. I now have a hygiene bag with some basic items that is ready to go if an emergency comes up again. Kathi's relatable writing and her humor sprinkled throughout will make you feel like your big sister is helping you prepare for things you may never have thought about before. Kathi helped me see how to be wise, not worried, about all the potential unexpected things life can bring.

Nicki Koziarz, two-time bestselling author
and speaker with Proverbs 31 Ministries

READY
FOR
ANYTHING

READY
FOR
ANYTHING

PREPARING YOUR HEART
AND HOME FOR ANY
CRISIS BIG OR SMALL

KATHI LIPP

**ZONDERVAN
BOOKS**

ZONDERVAN BOOKS

Ready for Anything
Copyright © 2020 by Kathi Lipp

Requests for information should be addressed to:
Zondervan, *3900 Sparks Dr. SE, Grand Rapids, Michigan 49546*

Zondervan titles may be purchased in bulk for educational, business, fundraising, or sales promotional use. For information, please email SpecialMarkets@Zondervan.com.

ISBN 978-0-310-35802-2 (audio)

Library of Congress Cataloging-in-Publication Data

Names: Lipp, Kathi, 1967- author.
Title: Ready for anything : preparing your heart and home for any crisis big or small / Kathi Lipp.
Description: Grand Rapids : Zondervan, 2020. | Summary: "There are those who've prepared, and those who wish they had. Let Kathi Lipp's Ready for Anything be your go-to guide for facing any unexpected crisis with confidence"-- Provided by publisher.
Identifiers: LCCN 2019052132 (print) | LCCN 2019052133 (ebook) | ISBN 9780310358008 (trade paperback) | ISBN 9780310358015 (ebook)
Subjects: LCSH: Preparedness. | Crisis management.
Classification: LCC HV551.2 .L57 2020 (print) | LCC HV551.2 (ebook) | DDC 613.6/9--dc23
LC record available at https://lccn.loc.gov/2019052132
LC ebook record available at https://lccn.loc.gov/2019052133

Published in association with the Books & Such Literary Agency, 52 Mission Circle, Suite 122, PMB 170, Santa Rosa, CA 95409-5370, www.booksandsuch.com.

Cover design: James W. Hall IV
Cover photos: Lunatictm / Shutterstock; Michela Ravasio / Stocksy
Interior design: Kait Lamphere

Printed in the United States of America

20 21 22 23 24 25 26 27 /LSC/ 15 14 13 12 11 10 9 8 7 6 5 4 3 2 1

This book is lovingly dedicated to my
super-agent, Rachelle Gardner.
Thank you for having the vision for this book and
your dogged determination to make sure that the
world is better prepared for everything in life.
Every time I write, I'm grateful that I have you
advocating for my words out in the world.

CONTENTS

ACKNOWLEDGMENTS

Thanks to Amanda and Shaun, Jeremy, Justen, and Kimberly for supporting your parents' crazy projects.

My team is the best collection of women on the planet. I'm grateful for all of you. Thanks to Tonya Kubo for leading our team and to Lyneta Smith for carrying me through the editing. You are the best book cheerleaders an author could ever have. And great thanks to the rest of our team's leaders for carrying on while our heads were down: Angela Bouma, Shantell Brightman, and Tiffany Baker.

Cheri Gregory, Susy Flory, and Michele Cushatt—thanks for talking me into the Red House and giving me the best stories.

Rachelle Gardner—thank you for believing more in this project than any other living human. Your faith made this project possible.

Stephanie Smith and the rest of the Zondervan team—so honored to be a part of your team. Thank you for fighting hard for the good stuff.

Connie Richerson—a mom who is supportive beyond love and common sense. So grateful for you.

And finally to Roger. Shut the door, baby.

INTRODUCTION

"Roger! We have to leave—*now!*"

I scoop up our thirty-eight-pound puggle, Jake, and head out the front door.

Once outside, we see why our neighbors are running from house to house, pounding on doors and yelling, "Fire! Fire! Fire!"

The town house two walls away from ours is totally engulfed in flames.

Our neighbors—a father and his two toddler boys—stand on the grass in front of their home, watching as the fire consumes their house.

As the flames start to overtake the house between ours and the fire, I start to imagine our home and everything in it being destroyed.

For the first time, I regret living in a town house as I recognize the risk because of what is happening just two doors down.

Suddenly my stomach seizes in panic.

"Roger, Jeremy didn't come home from school, did he?"

Jeremy is our kid who attends a local college. It's his first day of classes, and I'm not familiar with his schedule yet.

Roger thinks for a second, says, "No, we would have heard if he—" and then dashes back into our house.

Thirty long seconds later, both Jeremy and Roger emerge from our front door, both barefoot, Jeremy looking disheveled and a little more than slightly confused.

■　　■　　■

Roger would like it stated for the record that he's the dad who ran into a burning building to rescue his son.

But it's pretty hard to get around facts: we're the parents who grabbed the dog and left the kid in a burning building.

You see, apparently Jer had finished school and come home before his shift at work. Seeing that we were both busy, he didn't want to bother us and headed straight for his room and fell asleep—hard. The kind of sleep that only teenage boys can experience. The kind of sleep that is one step above "coma-like state." So hard, he didn't hear me or any of our neighbors yelling, "Fire!"

So, there we were, Roger, Jeremy, and I, all standing on our front lawn, barefoot, holding Jake the puggle (who was growing heavier by the minute). I had my cell phone, but otherwise, the only earthly possessions we had were the clothes we wore.

The firefighters arrived and worked on putting out the fire. They broke down the door to our next-door neighbor's home to insure no one was inside. Another neighbor found a dog leash so we could finally put Jake on the ground after half an hour.

Our neighbor's home? Gutted.

Our next-door neighbor's home? Fire, smoke, and water damage.

Our house? One hundred percent fine.

But we didn't know that for what seemed like hours. And in those first few minutes, we realized that we vastly over-estimated our ability to make good decisions in the midst of an emergency. We did dozens of things wrong for one simple reason: we assumed we would know all the right things to do when a crisis came. We assumed we would think straight, grab what needed to be grabbed, and get out of the house safely.

And we wrongly assumed that in a fire we would grab all the human family members.

Today if there is a fire, we have a plan. We know to grab these things:

- all the human family members (plus Jake)
- the fire box with cash and important documents in it
- our shoes (which we put in the same place every day so they are easy to find)
- our cell phones, which are always charging on our desks
- my purse and Roger's wallet by the front door
- the dog leash hanging by the front door
- the car keys, also by the front door

In addition to knowing what to grab, we have prepared in other ways as well:

- We have a small stash of emergency clothes in the car (a change of clothes, a sweatshirt, and a pair of shoes).
- All of our computer files are continually backed up to the Cloud, so if our computers are destroyed, all of our work is not.

- We have scanned our favorite photos and also store them in the Cloud, so if they are lost in a fire, they are not lost permanently.
- Our neighbors have our phone numbers, so if there is an emergency, they can contact us.
- One trusted neighbor has a key to our house in case of emergency so the firefighters don't have to take out the door like they did for our next-door neighbor, and can potentially get our dog out of the house if it's safe to do so.
- We know to leave the front door open so the cat can find her way out if we can't find her immediately.
- And most importantly, we know to check every room to make sure there are no sleeping kids.

The only reason we would do things differently today? We've thought through emergency situations and decided to do things differently.

For us, it took that one emergency to wake us up to the fact that we needed to be better prepared for unforeseen circumstances—emergencies we couldn't even imagine. We came out of our emergency relatively unscathed. But I had been through many other trying circumstances before the fire that pointed to my need to be better prepared:

- the gas shortages of the 1970s
- my dad's long-term unemployment while I was growing up
- the '89 earthquake in Northern California
- being completely broke while living in Uji, Japan, and having to go to the hospital

- being snowed in at a cabin for a week with two little kids and no car
- my first husband's long-term job loss
- going through a divorce and being unemployed
- being in a massive blackout that lasted for days while traveling
- being caught in a surprise snowstorm in Colorado

Your list of unforeseen circumstances may look nothing like mine, but one thing I can guarantee you: we will all have them. And while you can't predict what is going to happen or when, you can prepare for a variety of emergencies and unexpected situations.

In the past couple of years, our lives have changed pretty dramatically. Roger and I continue to run our business while he works a tech job in Silicon Valley. In addition to all of the regular chaos of living our lives, we have purchased a home in the mountains of Northern California where we live in the summer and winter. We host writing retreats for small groups and also host Airbnb guests during the tourist seasons (spring and fall). While we are living in the mountains, we rent out our house in San Jose on Airbnb. If you want to know just how unprepared you are, do two things: live in the mountains and rent your house out to other people.

While Roger and I have worked hard to get ready for anything, we have had to rediscover how much we don't know about being prepared (especially here in the mountains) and really work on our skills. To say that living prepared is a whole different way of life for us is truly an understatement.

Now, you need to know something about me. For decades

I actively resisted preparing for the unknown. I told myself that it was better just to "trust God" for any situation that came along. But after years of not preparing—and paying the price financially, emotionally, and physically in small crises and large emergencies alike—I realized that my attitude was less about trusting God and more about feeling completely overwhelmed. I was overwhelmed by the different disasters that could befall us. I was overwhelmed by all the preparations that needed to be made. I was overwhelmed by the time, money, and energy it would take to get prepared. So, instead of taking steps to prepare, I would fall back on "God will provide" and instantly get a mental check mark.

But my "just trust God" theology didn't really hold water. How was I trusting God when I constantly relied on other people to rescue me? How was I trusting God when I borrowed money when my tire got a hole in it or when I put an ER visit on my credit card?

In an emergency, whether it be a job loss, an earthquake, or some other disaster, I would much rather be in a position to help people than be the person in need of help.

THE PLAN-AHEADER VS. THE CATCHER-UPPER

I have lived most of my adult life looking in the rearview mirror.

While other people talked about plans they were making, I was always just barely catching up—and making excuses about why I wasn't keeping it all together.

I was the one who had a category in Quicken for "late fees" that was often bigger than my actual bills.

My first car ran out of gas more than a dozen times, requiring pushes to nearby gas stations because I didn't have a gas can. (Fortunately, it was a Honda Civic and was pretty easy to push.)

I was the one who always made excuses and felt like the world was out to get me because I could never seem to catch a break and get caught up.

If you are someone who has a bomb shelter in the backyard full of provisions and weapons, there's a good chance you also have a gas can in your car. This book is not for you. If you are someone who has written out a plan for every possible emergency scenario, this book is not for you.

But if you're tired of living on the edge . . . If you're tired of needing a miracle every day just to survive . . . If you want to be prepared, not *if* hard times hit, but *when* . . . If you've come to understand that planning for the future is biblical wisdom in action . . . If you are someone who longs to be ahead of the game instead of always catching up . . . This book is for you.

Some of us already know a crisis is coming or are already in the midst of one: we have seasonal work, a job that may be going away, medical expenses that are eating us alive, or some other circumstance that keeps us in need of a plan. And some of us will face emergencies that hit without any warning: a natural disaster, an injury that leaves us unable to work, a family crisis, a computer crash—just to name a few.

Much of our life is out of our control, but by preparing for hard times, or even for an emergency, well then, at least some of the results are in our control. And the feeling of going from always living in a deficit to getting "caught up," to actually facing and planning for the future? I can't even describe how empowering that is.

Going from the person who always needed rescuing, who always needed help, to having enough margin in my life that there are times I can be the person giving help? I can't tell you how much that has changed everything for me.

THE PROVERBS 31 PREPPER

When I started to write this book, the Proverbs 31 wife kept coming to mind. When I was a young wife, I hated the Proverbs 31 woman—I felt like she was an unreachable example of what we as women all needed to be—she was there to mock me in all my non-Proverbs31-ness. She was Wonder Woman, Florence Nightingale, and Oprah all rolled into one. Completely unobtainable.

But reading it again, now that I'm a little older (and hopefully a little wiser), I look at the list of all she accomplished and what it did for her, and it's certainly impressive:

- being an entrepreneur
- trading
- making investments
- farming
- sewing
- crafting
- managing servants
- serving the poor
- providing food for her family
- preparing for each season

She is one prepared woman.

And then I came to verse 25:

> "She is clothed with strength and dignity;
> she can laugh at the days to come."

To be someone who laughs at the days to come? Whoa. That stopped me in my tracks. To not fear the next bill or the next missed paycheck? To not fear the impending earthquake or flood? Not because those things won't happen to me but because I have taken wise steps and prepared myself and my family for the days to come? Now that's a woman I can get behind.

I've discovered that it's possible not only to have peace when facing the future but to stand up, hands on hips, and look at what is to come and laugh while saying, "That's right, I have God, I have wisdom, and I have two weeks' worth of food and water. Bring it!"

Because if there is one thing I know, it's that when the bad times come, big or small, the one thing in addition to our preparations we can control in an out-of-control situation is our attitude, and so much of our attitude is about laughing in the face of what is uncontrollable.

Recently, after rerouted flights, misplaced luggage, a flight that got delayed every hour on the hour, and a long night in an airport, I took a Lyft to the Philadelphia train station at three thirty in the morning. That was followed by a four-hour train trip to make it just in time to my speaking gig in Richmond, Virginia. I was tired. I was frustrated. I was not showered. But I made it.

The next morning, after a couple hours of sleep, I got to the airport to try to find my missing bag. After having to go through about eight people to actually get into the room where lost luggage goes to die, I found my bag, which had been on a whole adventure of its own. When we were reunited, I went back to the check-in desk, only to find that my flight had been canceled and I couldn't leave until the next day.

And I laughed.

Of course it had been canceled.

And when I laughed, the ticket agent said, "Well, that's not the response I usually get when I tell someone their flight has been canceled."

I let her know about the last couple of days.

"Where were you speaking at?" When I told her it was a church, she replied, "Well that's exactly why you're having all these problems! You are obviously filled with God's power, and there are forces in the world that want you to lose your witness. But don't you do it!"

It's not often that you get a full-blown sermon at the United counter.

Then she and three of her coworkers all worked together to get me on a patchwork of flights home that same day.

You cannot control your job. You cannot control the wind or the earth or the lightning or the clouds. But you can control your attitude. If you want to stop living in fear and be able to laugh at the days to come, this book, my friend, is for you.

CHAPTER ONE

WHAT READY FOR ANYTHING MEANS

(And What It Doesn't Mean)

It all started so innocently.

My husband, Roger, and I were on vacation in Canada. We are committed to living a simple and clutter-free life, so we each brought only one backpack and one carry-on suitcase for our sixteen-day trip. Neither of the Airbnbs we booked had laundry facilities, so for part of our vacation, I was stuck in a hot, ancient Laundromat waiting for our clothes to get clean and dry. This was not how I wanted to spend my precious time off.

I love to learn how to do new things, and I had plenty of time to consider alternatives to watching our clothes go around in circles, so I started to google "how to wash clothes without a washing machine."

Almost every article I read was from a "prepper" or "survivalist" website. I almost dismissed the whole idea, because sites like that, in my mind, were from people who lived in bunkers with a ten-year supply of canned stew. I wanted nothing to do with that kind of lifestyle. In fact, it freaked me out a little bit.

I eventually found articles about how to make your own "washing machine" with a bucket and an agitator. But I also read about how much water you should have on hand for an emergency, how to stock up on food without spending your entire paycheck, and how to plan for emergency backup lighting in case of a power outage.

I wondered if my vague notion of being prepared was doing me more harm than good. Sure, I had enough canned tomatoes to last me until Jesus comes back, but if all I had was one bag of pasta on hand, I was going to start wishing for his return after day three of eating cold tomatoes out of a can.

Even if I had plenty of food, without a supply of water, what good would rice or pasta do me if there was a disruption to the waterline? I live in earthquake country, so this is a real concern for us. But it could happen anywhere.

And sure, we have a grill to cook our meals on, but what if we didn't have the propane tanks full?

I was starting to see the flaws in my own preparedness. I started to buy a few extra cans of food on my monthly warehouse store shopping trip. My husband started to stock up on water. I made sure our emergency kit had everything we needed in case of, well, an emergency. Small things. Simple things. But each day I was closer to knowing that if an emergency happened, we were much better prepared than we were before.

And here's the thing: we did all this, pretty much, in secret. You see, whenever we discussed our desire to become more prepared, people had one of two reactions: (1) they thought we were crazy and offered to make us tinfoil hats out of the foil I'd stocked up on during our last Costco run, or (2) they were intrigued and wanted some basic ideas of how to be prepared themselves.

What I've noticed? More and more people are falling into category number two. They want to be prepared, but they just aren't sure of the next steps to take. And they feel completely overwhelmed by the whole idea, so it's easier just not to think about it than to start.

If that's where you are, my friend, you're not alone. For a long time, I resisted the urge to be prepared for a lot of reasons.

1. Am I really trusting God if I prepare for an emergency?
2. I don't want my life to be ruled by fear (which is what a lot of preppers use as currency).
3. How could I prepare for every situation?
4. I live most of the year in the suburbs. If something happens I can just call the police or fire department. Right?

But since that day at the Laundromat in Canada, I've realized that each of these points of resistance keeps me from being ready for the inevitable situation or disaster when—not if—it happens.

Let me unpack each one of these reasons and explain why they're faulty.

REASONS TO BE PREPARED

1. Am I Really Trusting God If I Prepare for an Emergency?

The argument I see most online against prepping is "Am I really trusting God if I prepare for an emergency?" Some would say, "If I trust God, and it's my time to go, then I'm okay with that. To be prepared means I'm not trusting God."

I feel that this argument is akin to saying, "Why take medicine? If I trust God, and it's my time to go, then I'm okay with that." Does taking medicine mean I'm not trusting God?

The Bible talks a lot about using wisdom in all situations and not being a fool. Proverbs 6:6–8 says, "Go to the ant, you sluggard; consider its ways and be wise! It has no commander, no overseer or ruler, yet it stores its provisions in summer and gathers its food at harvest." God has given us the ant as an example to demonstrate for us that his provision sometimes involves preparation and planning on our part.

2. I Don't Want My Life to Be Ruled by Fear.

Being prepared can come from one of two different places: wisdom or fear. I had to make sure my desire to be prepared wasn't trying to prepare all the fear away, which no one can really do. Instead, I wanted to be prepared enough to be wise, but not so much that I placed my trust for security in things rather than in God. When I really thought it through, I realized that what looked like wisdom was just fear with a Bible verse slapped on it. That is not how I wanted to live. When I do anything in my life to an extreme, it is usually fear showing up and calling itself by another name. So I had to make sure that my being prepared was not that.

When I do anything out of protecting myself, that's fear. But what I realized I really wanted to do was make sure that if there was a disaster, that I could take care of the people I love—and the people God has put around me. That is a place of wisdom and love.

I sometimes still find myself wanting to overprepare. I can now quickly recognize that as controlling behavior (fear with its Sunday school clothes on) and pray through the fear and work hard to get back to a place of peace. Fear pushes us into one extreme or another: either we just throw up our hands and say, "We'll just trust God," or we have to start dressing in camo and build a bunker in our townhome. I would like to think that I fall somewhere in between "Just trust God" and a ten-year supply of baked beans.

3. How Could I Prepare for Every Situation?

The idea of being prepared for every situation is what overwhelmed me at first. One major component of a disaster is the lack of foreknowledge that it's actually going to happen. How could I possibly be prepared for every scenario?

Of course, none of us can; that would be impossible. However, instead of preparing for a disaster, we can prepare for recovery after a disaster.

What do you need for recovery after any disaster? *Shelter*, *supplies*, and *cash*. That is why I advocate for 3-2-3: a three-day bug-out bag, two weeks of food and water, and three months of living expenses.

Now let's be clear—your uncle who watches *Doomsday Preppers* as if it were a college course? He will look at what you're trying to do here and scoff. He will guarantee all your preparing is just spitting in the wind, and that if a real disaster hits, you will never make it.

Let him spout his nonsense. Just know that while he's preparing for the end of the world as we know it, you are actually enjoying life right here and now. You know, the real world. Plus, you will be ready to face any problem like a boss.

Preparedness is not the opposite of trust. We prepare to the point of wisdom. I don't believe wisdom asks us to have twenty years' worth of food and water on hand and live in an underground bunker. But wisdom does dictate that we be prepared for what may come. When we have several days' worth of food and water on hand, we can make calm decisions when a crisis hits. Not only will we be ready ourselves but we will also have the ability to take care of our neighbors, family, and friends.

4. I Live Most of the Year in the Suburbs. If Something Happens, I Can Just Call the Police or Fire Department. Right?

Calling emergency responders in a crisis generally works fine—unless everyone around you is having a crisis at the same time. That's when you need to know how to take care of yourself and your neighbor until professionals can come to help.

But in most emergencies, first responders can't fix the core problem anyway. They don't have the means or the expertise to help with crises like broken waterlines or job loss.

While organizations like the Red Cross provide food, water, and shelter, they need time to get set up. We can't count on them in the immediate aftermath to provide for each need right away. And let's be real—their resources will only go so far.

Being ready for anything means that we'll have the power and resources to face emergencies or disasters when they come. I want to show you how you can get prepared without being overwhelmed. That's what *Ready for Anything* is all about.

HOW TO GET A RELUCTANT PARTNER ON BOARD

My prepping epiphany came while on vacation in the middle of a sorta-foreign country (Canada).

While Roger was open to the idea of being better prepared, the middle of the trip for which we had been saving (for years) was not the time my very patient husband wanted to hear about water tanks and learning CPR.

Roger eventually came around and not only embraced the prepping lifestyle but has stepped up and added to our plans. In the process, I learned that there is an art to getting loved ones on board.

If you are ready to start getting ready, but your spouse, roommate, kids, or anyone you live with is not, do not fear! Sure, you sound like a doomsday survivalist to them right now, but I bet that over time you can get them to join you in at least some of your prepping endeavors.

Start Small

This whole book is about taking small, doable steps. Do not unleash your whole plan on your partner at once. Start with small, commonsense steps that no one can argue with.

- Buy an extra four-dollar case of water to have on hand.
- Buy or update your first aid kit.
- Start filling up your car when the gas tank gets to half full (or half empty, depending on whether you are an optimist or a pessimist).

- Start putting away five dollars a week into an emergency fund by shopping sales and buying groceries in bulk.

Once you've done a few of these things, show your partner how you are already taking steps to be prepared, and demonstrate how simple and easy it is.

One of the main reasons people resist being prepared is that they think it will take a ton of effort, planning, and money. Demonstrate that while over the long haul it will require all of those things, taking these steps doesn't have to be daunting and will actually improve the quality of your life.

Lean on Your Partner's Strengths

For years, I asked my son (also a writer) to read Stephen King's *On Writing*. I knew he'd enjoy the book and get a lot out of it. Even though I suggested it numerous times, over several years, he never read it. Until, one day, he came to me and said, "Mom, you've got to read *On Writing* by Stephen King. It's so good!" (Cue mom suppressing a scream.)

You may experience a similar situation when it comes to prepping. If your spouse has been trying to get you to save money for years, and now you are finally ready because a book—even this one—told you to, your partner may be frustrated that you are finally ready to do something they have been talking about for years.

A better way to approach the topic is to let your spouse know that you see their point and that they were right all along and that you are now ready (it doesn't matter why) to get on board the saving train. If your spouse has a plan for saving, use their plan. I figure that if your spouse is already excited about a certain aspect of prepping (even if they don't see it as prepping), let them be in charge of that area and do it the way they see fit.

Whatever your partner's strengths, woo them to prepping using those strengths. Are they a great cook? Then have them help you figure out great meals using nonperishables. Handy around the house? Then talk about the desire to make needed repairs and do things like earthquake-proof furniture. Is your wife a computer genius? Then ask her to take charge of keeping all things internet related secure. If both of you do what you're great at, prepping will become a joy instead of a burden.

Only Do What You Can Do

My best piece of advice: do what you can do and keep having the conversation about being more prepared.

Control the things you're in control of. You have the power to create a first aid kit, come up with a disaster plan and post it in your house, and teach your kids what to do in an emergency. As your partner sees you being more and more prepared, I'm guessing they will want to add their two cents. Always invite collaboration. It will make your prepping more successful—and more fun—for everyone.

Timing Is Everything

Remember my epiphany during our epic vacation? That wasn't the time to start convincing my husband that we should prep.

You know your spouse and when it's a good time to discuss certain topics. Pick the time that is most conducive to convincing them to start getting ready for anything. Probably not during vacation, when the goal is to have downtime and relax. And probably not during an intense, stressful week when your family is busier than usual. Somewhere in between those extremes is the ideal time to start the conversation.

CHAPTER TWO

HOW TO PREP WITHOUT GETTING OVERWHELMED

If you are anything like me, when you first heard about the concept of prepping, you became overwhelmed just thinking about it.

You've seen the commercials, looked at the pamphlets, and maybe even attended a meeting where they talked about being prepared for a fire/flood/earthquake/tornado (fill in the blank, depending on where you live and your most likely emergency).

For years we were told to prepare for an earthquake, but we never really did because of one, simple fact: I was entirely overwhelmed. Gathering all that food and water? Strapping our furniture to the walls? It was just so much easier to hope that it wouldn't be that bad.

Sadly, hope is not a great emergency plan.

I completely get that this is a huge undertaking. It's not something most people even attempt. But it is something that could change (or save) your life.

One of the main reasons people resist being prepared is

because they feel there are so many things to do, they don't even know where to start. Just the thought of having to make lists and plan out what is needed seems like a monumental task. And then when I say, "Have three months' worth of expenses saved up," you want to fall into a crumpled pile of preparedness pamphlets and say, "I can't. I just can't."

I know it's a lot. I know it seems like an impossible feat. But, truly, there is only one thing you need to do: *be more prepared today than you were yesterday.*

That's it. Truly.

Will any of us be 100 percent prepared for any disaster that comes our way? No. That is impossible. But we can all be a little more prepared today than we were yesterday.

You can practice making a meal from shelf-stable goods for dinner tonight. Not only will you have dinner (score!) but you will have a new recipe in your arsenal and maybe learn that you don't have a manual can opener (which you can get the next time you're at the store so you will be ready if the power goes out).

And even though you may not have three months' worth of expenses saved up, you will have gained some knowledge and saved some money from eating from your stockpile.

By doing one simple act every day, you can refuse to be overwhelmed by the process and make huge strides toward being prepared for when an emergency hits.

Here are a few day-to-day ways to keep from being overwhelmed.

HAVE A PREP AND PLAN DAY

In my book *Overwhelmed*, with coauthor Cheri Gregory, I talk about having a prep and plan day each week. This is where I take a couple of hours and put into motion everything I want to get accomplished over the next week, month, and year.

Here are some examples of what tasks to complete on a prep and plan day:

- Make a dentist appointment for next month on your day off so the dentist can work with your schedule. (Taking great care of your teeth helps you be ready for anything so that you are not sidelined by pricey dental work or awful pain.)
- Create a shopping list for a big-box store. Add one shelf-stable item for your emergency pantry. (Adding an eight-pack of corn one week and a twelve-pack of pinto beans the next will quickly help you build up your pantry.)
- Schedule a first aid class for you and your family for the summer when you have more free time.
- Schedule one night this week to create a meal entirely from your pantry.
- Schedule a morning with your family to create a defensible space around your home by removing dead trees and bushes in case of fire.
- Schedule an emergency preparedness drill for your family.
- Check out your first aid kit and see what supplies you need to restock.
- Fill up your gas tank for the week.
- Keep an online wish list of emergency supplies, and order them on your prep and plan day as your budget allows.

- Create a binder to save your favorite recipes that you can use with only your pantry items.
- Spend fifteen minutes going through your pantry and getting rid of anything that has expired. (Or put a sticker on anything that should be used up quickly.)

Many of these things take just a few minutes to set into motion, but each of them will get you closer to being prepared than you were yesterday. You can absolutely do this.

REFRAME BEING PREPARED

Another reason you may feel overwhelmed by prepping is that it can be a downer of a topic. Who shows up at a party wanting to talk through the finer points of creating an emergency kit and a two-week stockpile of food? (Okay, I do. But that may mean that I'm not invited to your next party.)

But you see, I do not look at the process of being prepared as a doom-and-gloom proposition. I want to be prepared because I want to expand my capacity for joy and peace in my life.

Stay with me here.

I have come to understand that my soul craves simplicity. I look forward to preparing a home-cooked meal, playing a game of cards with my husband and some friends, sitting out on our porch with my dog and looking at the stars, and learning how to repair the dishwasher on my own. Some people might argue that if I really craved simplicity, I would love washing dishes by hand.

Let's not go crazy here, people.

The closer I get to a simple life, the closer I get to a prepared life. The more I learn to cook from scratch, the better prepared I am to cook when the power goes out for an extended time. The more water I have stored up, the less I have to panic when a pipe bursts and can't be fixed until next week. The more money I save by not buying things that only clutter up my life, the more money I will have when a disaster hits our family or someone we love.

Knowing I can care for myself and my neighbor in case of emergency means I can approach that relationship with peace and joy. I don't have to be consumed with "what ifs." I know that if a fire or earthquake hits, I have done what I can to take care of our family and our neighbors.

Being ready for anything ultimately helps us to avoid being overwhelmed and to enjoy peace of mind. We only have to move forward one step at a time.

CHAPTER THREE

ONE SIMPLE GOAL: GET TO 3-2-3

Life can be unpredictable. We never know when disaster or an emergency might strike. But we can know we're prepared. The best way to get there is step-by-step.

My goal with this book is to get you to 3-2-3:

THREE-DAY BAG: ready for three days if you must leave your house in an emergency

TWO-WEEKS' SUPPLY: two-weeks' supply if you need to stay in your house with no services

THREE-MONTH EMERGENCY FUND: ready for three months if you have a major financial crisis with no income

I showed this list to some of my team members who work in my ministry, and it induced a few small panic attacks. They thought I was crazy for preparing that much.

Seems like overkill? According to the Federal Emergency Management Agency (FEMA) and the Red Cross, it's not. In fact, this is exactly the minimum recommendation for preparation in the United States. And most financial planners recommend that you have six months' worth of emergency funds built up for a financial crisis. In fact, all of my recommendations are on the low side of what experts insist you need. But my feeling is that we all need to start somewhere.

If you already have a go-bag with a month's worth of provisions, a year's supply of food and water stored in your basement, and a six-month emergency fund, congratulations. You get a gold star and you don't need to read any further. But if you are like most people and your emergency kit consists of a couple of dried out Band-Aids and a flashlight with batteries covered in white gunk, please keep reading. Once you are at 3-2-3, you can decide if you want to keep building up your reserves.

When an emergency hits, are you going to refuse to help your favorite neighbor, adult kids who live nearby, or friends from church? What you thought was supplies for two weeks for you and your spouse may suddenly last three days for you and a few people you love.

Please don't get overwhelmed. You don't need to do this all in a day. In fact, as we go through this book, we are going to put building blocks in place so that you can accomplish a little at a time and know what you need to do next.

But for now, here is an overview of what we are going to accomplish together.

THREE-DAY BAG

Contained in the bag is everything you will need if you must leave your home in an emergency.

- food (lightweight, packaged foods that can be eaten without preparation, or just by adding water, are best)
- water (you can purchase water that comes in squeeze bags —think Capri Sun—to keep weight down in your pack)
- personal hygiene supplies (think personal wipes, a toothbrush and paste, feminine hygiene, deodorant, and lip balm to start)
- first aid kit (small, personal travel kits are available at Walmart)
- light source (flashlight, battery-operated lantern)
- mode of communication (walkie-talkies, cell phone backup battery)
- shelter and warmth (a small tent and sleeping bag for a single person or a sleeping bag for each family member and a tent big enough to hold the entire family)
- tools (Leatherman, garbage bags, matches, and heavy-duty gloves)
- paper evacuation maps (for when cell phone service is out)

Each member of your household, including any pets, will need their own three-day bag. Not everything has to be in every bag, but it works best if you decide the contents of each bag before an emergency, not in the midst of one.

TWO-WEEKS' SUPPLY

Some disasters could leave an entire area stranded without services for a couple of weeks. Hurricanes, earthquakes, and fires could mean closed roads or restricted travel.

In your home, you will want to have enough food, water, and supplies (toilet paper, battery-operated lights, ways to heat food, etc.) to stay self-sufficient for two weeks.

- water
- food
- manual can opener
- battery-powered or hand-crank radio for when cell phone service is out
- flashlights or other lighting sources
- prescription medications
- pet food and water
- first aid kit
- sanitation and personal hygiene items
- extra sets of car keys and house keys

THREE-MONTH EMERGENCY FUND

What if you or your spouse lost your job? What if you had a major medical emergency and insurance didn't cover all your expenditures?

There are so many financial disasters that can befall an individual or family, it's not worth taking up room in this book to scare you (and myself as I'm writing them down). So instead of being afraid, I want you to start working on your three-month emergency fund so that you don't need to concentrate on the "what ifs" and can start feeling financially secure enough to weather a bad patch or help someone you love when they have an emergency. When thinking about how much you will need, items to consider include the following:

- housing
- food
- utilities
- transportation
- debt

Other things that are part of your monthly budget can be cut immediately and do not need to be considered for an emergency budget:

- dining out
- entertainment
- clothes shopping
- vacation
- other savings goals

In the coming chapters, we'll talk about ways to increase your savings quickly so that you can build up your emergency fund.

This may sound like a lot, but here is the good news: you may be closer to these goals than you realize. Many of the items you need in your three-day bag can already be found in your home. Most of us have more food than we will eat just this week, so you are probably closer on the food front for the two-weeks' supply than you know. And we will talk about some doable ways to build your three-month emergency fund faster than you can imagine. The trick (especially for the three-day bag and the two-weeks' supply) is to gather everything you have together and know where it is so that in an emergency you aren't looking through boxes only to discover that the canned food you were thinking would get you through actually expired in 2007.

LEVERAGING YOUR 3-2-3

You may feel like you will never be able to do all three of these kinds of preparations at the same time. But realize this: once you've started to create one of these preps, you are starting on all three of them.

- When you have three days' worth of food in your three-day bag, that means you have three days' worth of food for the two-weeks' supply for staying at home.
- When you have money in your three-month emergency fund, you can put a bit of that cash in your home safe so that you have cash for your two-weeks' supply and for your three-day bag.

All of these preps leverage one another and build your safety overall.

Yes, it's going to take some time, energy, and money to accomplish your 3-2-3 goal. But the reward? The satisfaction of knowing that when a crisis hits, you're not at the mercy of the disaster. You planned for the days ahead and will not only survive but can help those you love to thrive in the process.

So let's get started.

FOUR

PREP #1: GET 100 ONE-DOLLAR BILLS AND A JUG OF WATER

As I've learned more about preparedness, others have asked me how to get started. At first I showed them my list of All. The. Things. You know—the hundred items everyone needs to survive any disaster anywhere (including a zombie apocalypse).

That's when I would see their eyes roll back in their heads and they'd start to mumble about "just trusting God when the big one hits" (which was especially surprising from my atheist relatives).

It turned out that my delivery needed a little work.

People want to be prepared. They know it's the wise thing to do, and they want to know that if something happens, they can take care of themselves and their families (and maybe even the neighbors they like). People are hungry for information, but in my zeal to make sure everyone I loved was A-OK, I overwhelmed them with way too much of it. And when people are overwhelmed, not only do they not complete a project, but it's hard for them even to get started.

READY FOR ANYTHING: GETTING THE FIRST CHECK MARK

Every day I have a list of things I want to get done—around the house, in my business, for my family. The list can seem daunting until I do the first thing and get the first check mark, and then suddenly I'm not staring at a giant list of to-dos but at a list of to-dos where I've already accomplished something.

One of the most powerful tools you can have in your ready-for-anything kit is the skill of getting the first check mark (i.e., starting a project), even if you start imperfectly. Only concern yourself with the first thing. Just get the first check mark.

One of the best things about getting the first check mark is that it gives you proof that you are capable. It gives you momentum to continue moving forward and puts a plan into action. Instead of analyzing the plan, you are executing the plan. You are in the midst of taking action. You go from being someone who is thinking about getting ready to someone who is actually getting ready.

Remember how, on my vacation, I discovered the world of prepping and couldn't stop reading and planning about all the things I was going to do to get ready for anything?

Yeah . . . well . . .

Reading and planning were all I did for a while.

Prepping just seemed like such a huge commitment. Was I really going to go all in on this prepping stuff? Was I going to be the neighbor who, when we lifted our garage door, displayed enough jugs of water and canned food to feed a small neighborhood? Were we really going to be those people?

And then I did it. I bought the water tanks. It felt weird and subversive and like I was on the show *Doomsday Preppers*. But I did it.

Before buying the tanks, I remember thinking, *Well, if I can't do everything right away, why do anything at all?* I had a million excuses for not getting started. But once I finally did buy the water tanks, I felt empowered. *Well, that was easy. And I did it! What's next?*

I want you to feel empowered. Right away.

Do the first weird thing. Right now. Go buy the water tanks. I recommend the Reliance Products Aqua-Tainer 7 Gallon Rigid Water Container.

Really. I'll wait.

Done?

Okay. Now don't you feel awesome? Don't you feel like you can handle anything? Because you, my friend, have water tanks on the way.

You are now officially more prepared than you were yesterday. Amazing!

There is power in checking something off a to-do list, and when you check off the first thing, it is so much easier to move on to the second thing, and then the third, and eventually you become someone who is actually prepared.

This getting the first check mark concept is applicable in all areas of our lives. James 1:22 says, "Do not merely listen to the word, and so deceive yourselves. Do what it says." How often do we talk about biblical concepts, and they are great in theory, but we never do anything about them? We talk about starting a savings plan for the future or starting to read the Bible, and we get caught up in how big the task is, so we never get started. It's so much easier to talk about what to do than to actually do it. But getting started can help us do what we need to do instead of just knowing what we need to do.

Developing the discipline to start a task, even imperfectly, will help us in every area of our lives.

So I have now officially softened my approach, and instead of doing my Chicken Little impersonation when someone asks me about getting prepared, I quietly and lovingly encourage them to do two simple things: get 100 one-dollar bills and fill up a jug of water.

Why those two to-dos?

1. 100 One-Dollar Bills

You will never regret having extra money on hand, no matter the situation. One time Roger and I were on vacation and the area we were in lost all power. Our debit and credit cards were useless. We couldn't get money out of the ATM, and we had less than fifty dollars cash to our name. Oh, and we were low on gas. Swell.

Having cash on hand would have given us more options. We could have bought the gas we needed. We could have eaten lunch and bought some food for later.

The same holds true for you. Having 100 one-dollar bills will give you options. (I like small bills so that if someone isn't able to make change, you aren't paying twenty dollars for a can of soda.) If power is down and you want to fill up your tank, most stations have transfer switches installed or generators on hand so you can still get gas when the power is down, even if they can't use their credit card readers. You can also pay someone to shovel your driveway, pay for ice at the local convenience store, and pay for a prescription that is waiting for you at the drugstore.

If all your power went out and you couldn't use your debit card, how much cash would you have on hand? While one hundred dollars isn't going to hold you for days on end, it's a great start.

Plus, cash is just handy to have around. When I want to tip the food delivery guy, reimburse a friend who stopped at the store for me, or pay the kid across the street who took my dog for a walk while I worked late, I can pay them quickly and easily (and replenish the cash the next time I go to the store or bank).

In an emergency, cash is always your best option—even if it's just meeting a friend at the hospital and needing money for the vending machine while you wait for her to be seen. In an emergency, people don't want your Bitcoin or your money from a new app they have to download. Cash is king.

If you already have a hundred dollars in the bank, great. Just go there and ask for it in one-dollar bills. This is a common practice; I do it for my business almost every other month. Don't have a hundred dollars available right now? Here are a couple of ways to start collecting that money:

1. Over the next five weeks, scale back a little on your grocery shopping and get twenty dollars in ones at the checkout.
2. If you have a change jar, run that money through a Coinstar machine and see how close you are to one hundred dollars.

3. See if you can sell something to get the cash—a bike you don't use, a gaming system, a piece of exercise equipment you had the best of intentions for but never got around to using.

4. Take your lunch to work two days a week instead of buying it. In five to six weeks you will have saved over one hundred dollars.

5. Instead of ordering Friday night pizzas from your favorite pizzeria, make pizza at home. It's actually pretty fun to do. Over a couple of weeks you will have saved at least one hundred dollars.

6. Refrain from buying clothes for a month. Spend the time you would have spent at the mall shopping your own closet and putting together new outfits. I like to look at Pinterest to see what clothes I already have that are featured in "looks" there and see how I can recreate those looks at home. Use the money you would have spent on clothes to create your one-hundred-dollar stash.

7. Turn your hobby into a moneymaker. My friend Becky is an excellent baker and has a group of people who line up every year at Easter to buy her homemade scones. She makes an announcement on Facebook, and people place their orders. The trick is that she only does it once or twice a year, making the "more-than-you'd-pay-at-the-supermarket" scones a special treat because they're scarce. What do you love to do that other people would pay for, just this once, so that you can earn that one hundred dollars?

8. Skip the coffee shop and make your coffee at home for a month or two. But if you love coffee like I do, this is only as a last resort. We don't want to go crazy here.

2. A Jug of Water

We live in a town house complex where every time someone on our block needs to have repairs made to their water system, all the water has to be shut off. These times have been great reminders to me of how reliant I am on water coming out of that tap each time I turn it on (not to mention for washing clothes and the luxury of flushing).

In a true emergency, our most precious resource, most likely, will be clean water. Every emergency preparedness site, book, and pamphlet recommends one gallon of fresh water per person per day for drinking, cooking, cleaning, and washing clothes. Eventually you'll need to acquire several jugs for yourself and your family, but for now, I want you to get just one jug of water to start.

The Reliance Products Aqua-Tainer is sturdy and square, making it easy to stack and store as you grow your reserves. Reliance Products says they should only be stacked when empty, but ours are stacked two up when full, and we have never had a problem. When storing water, remember that if you are storing in an area that is prone to freezing (garage, basement), do not fill the jug up all the way as water expands as it freezes.

In chapter 13 we will talk about how to store water safely, but for now I just want you to get the tank so you can get your check mark.

Simple, right? Yes, you are just starting out, but you will keep building and building your preparedness. Eventually you will get to 3-2-3. But just by doing these two things, you will already be much better prepared to handle whatever emergency comes your way.

YOUR PLAN

Grab a notebook for your ready-for-anything plans and keep track of your readiness projects.

Write out your specific plan for getting your 100 one-dollar bills together and buying your water storage jug. There's nothing like a due date to keep you motivated, so set a deadline to finish your goal.

I'm proud of you for taking this first step. And now that you've started, let's keep getting those check marks!

CHAPTER FIVE

PREP #2: MAKE A FIVE-MINUTE PLAN

When is the worst time to decide what to do in an emergency?

When the emergency hits.

As someone who watches all kinds of "emergency" shows on TV—*ER*, *Chicago Med*, *Hill Street Blues*, *Grey's Anatomy*, *M*A*S*H*—I always thought that when something bad happened, I would get my hero on and do the right thing. I had the secret thought that if my kid were pinned under a car, I'd be able to lift a Toyota Sienna minivan to get her out from underneath.

But as my story about how Roger and I reacted during the fire teaches, most of us temporarily lose our minds in the midst of a crisis. Our emotions make us stupid. And that is why the concept of *prediciding* is so vital.

Prediciding is when you make a decision before you get into the thick of a situation. It can be as simple as making a menu plan for the rest of the week so you don't get to five thirty each night and have to figure out what in the world you are going to make for dinner. Or it can be as hard as deciding that the next time I see Aunt June and she mentions how much weight I've gained—because she lives for that kind of thing—I'm going to say, "So good to see you," and then give my husband the preagreed-upon signal to get me out of there.

Predeciding takes most of the emotion out of decisions because we are not in the midst of the situation. We can use logic and wisdom instead of adrenaline and anxiety. And that will make our decisions—for us and our family—so much better, healthier, and wiser.

One of the biggest benefits of predeciding is giving ourselves and our loved ones the confidence that if something scary happens, we have a plan.

One of my favorite stories of predeciding is about Daniel in the Old Testament. When the tribe of Judah was captured by Babylon, several of the young men were singled out to work for Nebuchadnezzar, king of Babylon. In the midst of their training, they were given the best food and wine so that they would stay fit and healthy during their time of learning.

But Daniel resolved not to defile himself with the royal food and wine, and he asked the chief official for permission not to defile himself this way. Now God had caused the official to show favor and compassion to Daniel, but the official told Daniel, "I am afraid of my lord the king, who has assigned your food and drink. Why should he see you looking worse than the other young men your age? The king would then have my head because of you."

Daniel then said to the guard whom the chief official had appointed over Daniel, Hananiah, Mishael and Azariah, "Please test your servants for ten days: Give us nothing but vegetables to eat and water to drink. Then compare our appearance with that of the young men who eat the royal food and treat your servants in accordance with what you see." So he agreed to this and tested them for ten days.

At the end of the ten days they looked healthier and better nourished than any of the young men who ate the royal food. So the guard took away their choice food and the wine they were to drink and gave them vegetables instead. (Daniel 1:8–16)

I can only imagine how hard it would have been to refuse all those meats, honey, and grains in the heat of the moment. But Daniel resolved in advance not to be subject to the king. He "predecided," and God not only honored his choice but made Daniel and his friends healthier than those around them who were eating all the royal foods.

Throughout the Bible we see God honoring those who made decisions before they were ever tested who remained faithful to their plans.

Here are some other examples:

RUTH 1: When Ruth decides to stay with Naomi, even though her husband has died and Naomi has nothing to offer Ruth.

DANIEL 3: Shadrach, Meshach, and Abednego, who refused to bow down to the king's image and were thrown into the fiery furnace but were preserved from harm.

ESTHER 4: When Queen Esther went before the king and made an appeal for the lives of the Jewish people, she declared, "Go, gather together all the Jews who are in Susa, and fast for me. Do not eat or drink for three days, night or day. I and my attendants will fast as you do. When this is done, I will go to the king, even though it is against the law. And if I perish, I perish" (v. 16).

LUKE 10: Mary choosing to sit at Jesus's feet even though she was receiving pressure from Martha to get up and help with the preparations.

PHILIPPIANS 4: Paul's decision to focus on God, and not his circumstances, while in prison awaiting trial.

These are just a few of the circumstances where God empowered people to set a course and follow it, despite hardship and temptations to choose a different route.

Predeciding is an invaluable skill. Making a decision about how you will act before a crisis comes will save you pain and heartache in everything from parenting to budgeting, to handling an emergency. For example, how will you act when your kid comes home with a D? How will you pay for a new transmission when your car dies? How will you get your ninety-pound German shepherd to the vet if it gets injured?

Most of the preps we are going to talk about in this book involve some form of predeciding, but for no other prep is it more important than this one: what you do in the first five minutes of a crisis.

Think through what you would do in the first five minutes after your most likely emergency, and then discuss it with the people you live with. For us, the two most likely emergencies are job loss and earthquake (because we live in California).

If Roger came home and told me he had been laid off, my reaction, before coming up with a five-minute plan, would have been to cry and panic. (My dad was unemployed much of my childhood, and my first husband went through extended times of unemployment, so job loss is a tender spot in my life.) Crying and panicking would only have added insult to injury for Roger, I'm sure. In an earthquake, my reaction before coming up with my five-minute plan would have been to call all my kids to see if they were okay. Some of my kids work as teachers and emergency responders, so that would have been a complete waste of time because they have to protect the people they are charged with caring for, not answer panicked calls from their mommy.

Now, because my husband and I have developed our five-minute plans, our responses have a higher likelihood of being planned, not panicked.

Our five-minute plan following a job loss:

1. Sit down and pray together.
2. **ROGER:** Start the process of liquidating some of our emergency fund for the next couple of months.
3. **KATHI:** Cancel optional services to save money.

Are those emergencies in this situation? Not necessarily. What I love is that we have actionable plans. We have some things to do instead of worrying. We can start to take control of the situation immediately and feel empowered to help our situation.

Our five-minute plan following an earthquake (conditions allowing):

1. **ROGER:** Grab car keys and gas up both cars and buy extra propane from the gas station around the corner.
2. **KATHI:** Fill bathtub with water. Check on pets (get cat inside if she's outside). Check on our older neighbor to see if she's okay.

If you have kids, make sure they have a plan for the first five minutes as well. It's easy for kids to become overwhelmed and fearful in an emergency situation, feeling helpless and unsure. But if your kids have a job to do, they can be focused and contribute to the rest of the family.

If your kids are at school or with a childcare worker, they are probably safest where they are for the moment. Their job is to listen to their adult in charge and help as much as they can.

If your kids are at home, having a list of jobs they can do to help the family will empower them.

Things kids can do right after an emergency (depending on age and capability):

1. Count all the money in the family coin jar to see how much you have. Those coin jars can add up!
2. Fill buckets with water.
3. Take an inventory of food and water.
4. Make sure all phones, tablets, and computers are charging if you still have electricity.
5. Check on neighbors.
6. Make a meal (even if it's peanut butter and jelly sandwiches) while Mom and Dad take care of business.
7. Put fresh batteries in flashlights.
8. Find paper plates, cups, and plasticware.

Decide now what you will do in the first five minutes after a crisis hits. It's one of the most powerful things you can do now to take care of yourself and your family later.

THINK OF YOUR FIVE-MINUTE PLAN AS A KINDNESS TO YOUR FUTURE SELF

As you may remember from the opening of this book, Roger and I did not have a five-minute plan when the fire hit our town house complex. That is when panic, unpreparedness, and leaving an almost-adult child asleep in bed during a fire happened. Not the way I wanted to respond in an emergency.

I know that my resisting of planning ahead comes from not wanting to make hard decisions. How do I actually say aloud that if we can't find the cat during a fire, we leave the door open and hope for the best? But, if I've thought through that particular scenario in advance, I can make the decision that is best for me and for Ashley and not spend precious minutes hunting her down and possibly putting myself or my loved ones in danger.

You will want to have a five-minute plan for getting out of the house in an emergency, but there are other scenarios for which a five-minute plan could be a lifesaver—literally and figuratively. For example, just yesterday I made one of the hardest but most likely five-minute plans I will need—euthanizing our dog, Jake. Yes, it's about to get a little dark here, but stick with me.

Our puggle, Jake, has been the weirdest and best dog I've ever had. Our other dogs were my parents' dogs or my husband's dog, but Jake is my dog—I am Jake's primary human. Roger comes in a very close second, but I am the person who primarily feeds him, so I get the most love. Everyone else is just a backup human to Jake.

We've had Jake since he was a little over two, and from what we can tell, he was not well cared for as a youngster. He is a bit quirky—not something every potential dog owner looks for—so when we adopted him from the animal shelter, it was our job to make sure that he was well loved.

At the age of fifteen, Jake has outlived every other puggle we know. We are sure the end is near, and we are loving every smelly minute we get with Jake. But I know that when his time comes, I will be a mess, as evidenced by my bawling as I typed that last sentence. (Jake has put a paw on me, as if to say, "Don't be sad, Mommy. I know what will make you feel better: go get me a jerky treat!")

Yesterday I spent thirty minutes thinking through my five-minute plan for when the time to say goodbye comes:

1. I researched and contacted a local vet who makes house calls for such situations. The vet's number is in my phone and in our binder for dog sitters. While we live in the mountains, our vet is about forty-five minutes away, and we would prefer not to have to take Jake in the car when he's in distress.

2. I've made arrangements for his remains, so it's not something I have to do in the moment. The vet knows what needs to happen without even asking me.

3. I've predecided that we will have a little money set aside so that when he passes we can do two things:
   a. Have his pawprint cast for a stepping-stone up here in the mountains.

b. Help another family who can't afford the initial adoption fees and other expenses so they can enjoy having a dog (e.g., a crate, bed, licensing, and any veterinarian procedures). We will do that in Jake's honor.

Jake's death is a hard thing to think about now, but when the time comes, having a plan will make the situation just a little bit easier for Roger and me, and hopefully for Jake.

You can figure out a five-minute plan for any situation you dread. Instead of living in fear, exercise some power and apply purpose to your predeciding. It's not fun in the moment, but if the time should ever come that you need a five-minute plan, you'll be so relieved that you created one. Be kind to your future self.

YOUR PLAN

Write down your agenda for a family meeting in your Ready for Anything notebook and schedule it on the calendar; include everyone who will have a role in the first five minutes after an emergency. Don't forget to set a deadline to finish writing your five-minute plan.

A big part of reducing anxiety is having a plan. Predeciding what you'll do in an emergency will give your family the confidence they need to continue getting ready for anything.

PREP #3: IDENTIFY YOUR DISASTER

I discovered that one of the most overwhelming things about prepping was that it felt like the books and guides I was reading were trying to get me prepared for any and every emergency. But here's the good news for me—I don't have to spend a lot of time worrying about hurricanes here in Northern California. The bad news? There are plenty of other disasters I need to be prepared for: wildfires, floods, snowstorms, earthquakes. And those are just natural disasters. A whole slew of other disasters can happen to anyone, wherever they live: unemployment, illness, an accident, a house fire.

Recognizing what disasters are most likely to befall you and what preps you can make for them is vital. For instance, in our town house in San Jose, California, one of the most likely disasters is a major earthquake. I've grown up with earthquakes my entire life. In school we would have regularly scheduled earthquake drills, but that was the extent of the preparedness I had in my life. Then, as a young adult, I moved to Japan, where earthquakes are an everyday occurrence. Again, I never thought of being prepared for those quakes, even though I lived on the fourth floor of an apartment building that had the structural integrity of a piñata.

When I was twenty-two, the Bay Area earthquake of '89 changed everything. The shaking and rolling of this 6.9 magnitude quake seemed like it would never stop. It was truly one of the most terrifying moments in my life. This was before cell phones were smaller than the side of a lunch box, and I couldn't get ahold of people I loved. Some were at the World Series in San Francisco, while most were just getting off work. All we could see were the news reports of downed buildings and the collapsed Nimitz Freeway, a double-decker freeway.

That was the first time I heard people talk about being more prepared than just finding a table to crawl under. We finally bolted heavy furniture to the wall so that bookcases wouldn't fall down on our heads during the next earthquake.

Another prep for earthquakes is to have your water plan in place (one gallon per person per day for two weeks), since for many homes, water service will be disrupted after an earthquake.

I know this seems like a lot to prepare for all at once. The good news is that when you store water for survival after an earthquake, you are also storing it for survival after a snowstorm. And when you save up money for surviving after a hurricane, you are also saving up money to survive after a job loss. Let's be honest: almost anything could happen anywhere. We learned this when San Jose experienced a flood in 2018, something I had never seen in my forty-plus years of living here. But instead of prepping for everything, pick the most likely scenarios for your area and situation, and prepare for those.

As I mentioned earlier, we have a house in San Jose (Silicon Valley, very much the suburbs), and we have another in Somerset (very much the mountains). We have to prepare differently for each of those homes. For San Jose I need to prep for earthquake, fire, and life circumstances (such as job loss or illness). In Somerset we have more opportunities for natural disasters, with wildfires being the biggest threat, followed closely by flooding and snowstorms.

From the list of natural disasters below, choose which ones are most likely to affect you in your area:

hurricane	mudflow	landslide
wildfire	cold wave	earthquake
flood	snowstorm	drought
blizzard	tsunami	volcano
tornado	heat wave	

When you focus on the disasters mostly likely to happen in your area, you won't be overwhelmed by every possible disaster known to man. You'll be able to concentrate on making the preparations you need the most.

YOUR PLAN

Write in your notebook your plan for the emergencies most likely to happen in your area, plus contingencies common to us all.

CHAPTER SEVEN

PREP #4: TAKE A THREE-DAY BAG INVENTORY

In November 2018 Roger and I had booked a family to stay at our Somerset home through Airbnb for a fortieth birthday celebration. We spent some extra time making sure that everything was as close to perfect as possible for this special celebration, and then we got out of the house a couple of days early to get back to our home in San Jose.

Unexpectedly we received a message over the Airbnb platform. "Hey Kathi, we are excited about our trip, but a change of plans has come up. We live in Chico near the Camp Fire in Paradise. We've been told to evacuate, and our cars are packed. Is there any way we can come up early?"

I told the family to come, of course. We had been watching the fires on the local news and felt helpless to offer assistance. It felt great to offer tangible help in such a desperate time.

Our guests were given eight hours' notice to grab everything they needed for the next few days or months. They didn't know if their house would be standing when they returned. Some people had only minutes to decide what to take. This is why it's important to have a three-day bag packed and ready to go.

Trying to decide what to take in the heat of the moment is an overwhelming task. Our guests had a safe place to go that included necessities like toothbrushes, toothpaste, shampoo, conditioner, an emergency stockpile of food, and a washing machine and dryer to wash clothes. But preparing to live outside of your home for three days in the case of an emergency is different than packing for a three-day trip—or packing for a three-hour tour like the gang who landed on Gilligan's Island (apparently, Mrs. Howell and Ginger each "Hollywood packed" and had changes of clothing for every occasion).

Packing a three-day bag isn't simply packing clothes for three days and then making reservations for the California Pizza Kitchen while on the road.

What if your house (along with hundreds or thousands of other homes in your area) was damaged?

What if everyone in your area was trying to get out of town to find shelter?

What if grocery stores were closed or their shelves were cleared out?

What if you had to sleep in your car for a couple of nights until different arrangements could be made?

What if a situation came up where you couldn't sleep in your house for a few nights and you either didn't have money to pay for a hotel or hotels wouldn't accept your credit or debit card?

All of these scenarios are possibilities (and it takes just one or two things going wrong for them to become realities for some). That's why you need a three-day bag, more commonly referred to as a "bug-out bag," or BOB. A bug-out bag has everything you would need to survive somewhat comfortably for three days without being able to get into your home.

In an emergency, you may not know when you will be able to get to a friend's house to take shelter or which of the roads out of your area will be closed. By having a bug-out bag, you give yourself the gift of creating some time to make smart decisions and come up with a plan.

One of the big concepts we will focus on throughout this book is the idea of prediciding. As I mentioned before (and it bears repeating), making decisions in the midst of a crisis is hard. While upset and panicked, you may potentially be making choices that will impact your family for a while to come. So prediciding—making decisions when you're calm—is far better.

You will need a bag for every member of your family (even furry members). Extreme preppers will tell you all the things you need to have in your bug-out bag to survive in the wilderness for days on end. They will let you know that your bag isn't complete without fire starter and a handgun. I am going to go a little more basic than that.

THE BAG

You will want to have a bag that is easy to carry. We each have a backpack for our own bug-out bag, and a small duffel bag each for our dog and cat. We hope we would be able to take our car in an emergency, but if not, it's good to know that we could walk for a while with our bags.

The temptation is to get a giant bag to put all your things

in. Resist the temptation. Take just the essentials that you can carry by yourself, or if you have a physical limitation, make a plan for how your bag will get where it needs to go.

If you have a backpack lying around the house, start with that one. As long as you can wear the backpack, this will at least get all of your supplies into one place and will give you an idea of what size bag you will need. It is helpful to have a bag with extra pockets or carabiner hooks for things like water bottles or other small necessities.

Here is a list of items recommended by the Red Cross[1] that you will need in your bag (some of this will depend on your own set of circumstances, the weather where you live, etc. Use common sense when packing what you need.):

- water: one gallon per person, per day (3-day supply for evacuation, 2-week supply for home)
- food: nonperishable, easy-to-prepare items (3-day supply for evacuation, 2-week supply for home)
- flashlight
- battery-powered or hand-crank radio (NOAA Weather Radio, if possible)
- extra batteries (Similar item available in the Red Cross Store)
- deluxe family first aid kit
- medications (7-day supply) and medical items
- multipurpose tool
- sanitation and personal hygiene items

---

1. Survival Kit Supplies, https://www.redcross.org/get-help/how-to-prepare -for-emergencies/survival-kit-supplies.html.

- copies of personal documents (medication list and pertinent medical information, proof of address, deed/lease to home, passports, birth certificates, insurance policies)
- cell phone with chargers (similar item available in the Red Cross Store)
- family and emergency contact information
- extra cash
- emergency blanket
- map(s) of the area

Consider the needs of all family members and add supplies to your kit:

- medical supplies (hearing aids with extra batteries, glasses, contact lenses, syringes, etc.)
- baby supplies (bottles, formula, baby food, diapers)
- games and activities for children
- pet supplies (collar, leash, ID, food, carrier, bowl)
- two-way radios
- extra set of car keys and house keys
- manual can opener

Additional supplies to keep at home or in your survival kit based on the types of disasters common to your area:

- whistle
- N95 or surgical masks
- matches
- rain gear

- towels
- work gloves
- tools/supplies for securing your home
- extra clothing, hat, and sturdy shoes
- plastic sheeting
- duct tape
- scissors
- household liquid bleach
- entertainment items
- blankets or sleeping bags

YOUR PLAN

Write a list of things you need to buy for your three-day bag in your Ready for Anything notebook. Refer to the list on page 43 to get you started.

Set a deadline and put a day on the calendar to go to the store.

Once the bug-out bags are packed, make sure each member of the family knows where the bags are kept. Make a plan for who will grab each BOB (e.g., who is going to carry the pets' bags?).

EIGHT

PREP #5: TAKE A FINANCIAL INVENTORY

Whether earthquake, flood, fire, or job loss, the one thing disasters have in common is that they impact their victims financially.

My biggest fear is that you will discover the truth about your finances in the midst of a disaster rather than before. And if you are embarrassed about where your finances currently stand, let me put your heart at rest: no matter how bad your finances are, you can make progress. None of us is beyond hope. It's just that for some of us, hope is a little further out than it is for others.

For most of my life, I was a financial disaster. I would spend money I didn't have on things I didn't need, only to be on the financial edge (and sometimes falling off the cliff) anytime anything went wrong.

I was the girl who would put four dollars' worth of gas in my car. Fortunately, this was the '90s, so four dollars' worth of gas in my Honda Civic would last a few days. But still—four dollars?

I was in such denial that if I had to look at my bank

balance, I would do it like a sixth grader at a scary movie: hands covering my eyes, slowly separating my fingers to see the scary balance (often with a minus sign in front of it).

I had massive credit card debt; I was maxed out in every way possible.

So when something huge hit (like my first husband losing his job) or tiny (like the library late fees I was so adept at amassing), my life went from zero to crisis in the swipe of an ATM card.

The good news is that if someone with the financial disaster I had could face her financial future, you can too. Because while discovering the facts can be scary, and even crushing, the actual information, once you have it, is not only motivating but can be truly powerful.

When you're living blissfully unaware of your true circumstances, you can't make any progress. But once you assess the truth, hopefully you will either be excited about where you are financially and feel empowered to make progress toward preparing for a crisis. Or you will see the precariousness of your situation and vow to stop living on the financial edge and begin to make sacrifices to change the trajectory of your financial life. So before we start talking about moving on from your one-hundred-dollar emergency stash and saving some real cash, it's important to know where you stand.

If you're afraid to assess your financial situation, knowing the truth about your finances and making small steps toward getting financially healthy is a lot more peace-filled than ignoring the situation and hoping it goes away. Because while credit card companies may forget to credit you, they will never, ever forget to bill you. They are on top of things like that.

So how do you go about knowing where you stand financially?

One of my favorite resources is *The Total Money Makeover* by Dave Ramsey. This book will help you make an accurate assessment of your finances and give you some great steps to recover from past financial mistakes and get back to even ground.

Why is it so important to know where you stand? So that you can initiate a plan to save for the next unforeseen event that comes up. And when you know how much money has to go toward paying off credit card debt, mortgage or rent, food, utilities, clothing, and other necessities, you can make the hard decisions for yourself and your family. This is the time to use all your God-given creativity and figure out ways not only to save money but also to earn money to help you get to your financial goals.

Here's a breakdown of some ready-for-anything financial goals:

1. Save up one hundred dollars in one-dollar bills. (The great news is that you have either done this or have already made a plan to check it off your list!)
2. Take a financial inventory.
3. If you have debt, start to pay off the bill with the lowest balance first.
4. At the same time you are paying off debt, start building your emergency fund. Your first goal is to save a buffer fund of $1,000.
5. Keep paying down debt.
6. Continue building up your emergency fund until you have enough saved to cover three months' worth of expenses as outlined in the 3-2-3 plan (see chapter 3).

The key is to create some small goals for yourself. Please don't look at this list and get overwhelmed. This is not a weekend project. For many of us, this whole list, if we are already out of debt and have savings, could still take us months. For some of us, it may take years. Don't get discouraged. Every single step you take will help you get closer to being prepared when an unexpected circumstance happens.

Here is an example of a list of small goals to consider:

1. PAY OFF A CREDIT CARD. FOR EXAMPLE, PAY OFF YOUR HOME IMPROVEMENT STORE CREDIT CARD BALANCE OF $596.

How I will accomplish this:
- Pay $120 a month over the next six months (last payment will be less).
- Find three hours of work I can do each week to bring in the necessary income: babysitting, editing a friend's blog, graphic design, housecleaning, yard work, decluttering and organizing other people's garages, or something else.

2. SAVE $300 FOR THE $1,000 EMERGENCY FUND.

How I will accomplish this:
Every week, I will come up with a way to cut expenses so I can save fifty dollars or ways I can earn fifty dollars.

Save-fifty-dollars ideas:
- Rededicate yourself to cooking. When life gets busy, it's easy to fall into the habit of letting a wholesale store

do your catering. And while no one loves a Costco deal more than I do, it is not the cheapest way to feed a family. Use a prepared cheat meal for the days you would be tempted to use a drive-through, and then on the days where you have a little more leeway, plan your meals ahead to take the stress out of getting dinner on the table. (A plan, even on the back of an envelope, will cut down half the angst of getting dinner ready and save you money too.)

- Grocery shop according to the sales. Each week, take your grocery store flyer and check out the loss-leaders (items the grocery store is selling on the front page to attract customers). This is usually the best deal of the week and something you may want to consider stocking up on. At least once a month, my local grocery store will have whole chickens (much cheaper than buying parts) on sale. I wait until that is the loss leader and then buy four or six at a time. (When my kids were at home, I was known to buy eight at a time.) Usually once a week we will have roasted chicken for dinner and then use the leftovers (we have leftovers now that we don't have two teenage boys living with us) to make Greek yogurt chicken salad or chicken and rice soup. Most of the time we can get three meals out of one chicken, which stretches our grocery budget further than almost anything else we can buy on sale.

- Cut the mall habit. In 2017 I challenged myself to buy only twelve pieces of clothing throughout the year. (Yes, that included shoes, undergarments, and accessories.) I was doing it as a clutter-free challenge, but what

I realized is that the clothing I purchased was not only taking up space in my home but impacted our bottom line as well. Give yourself a strict budget of how much you will spend on clothing, and then get creative with what you already have.

- Use up your gift cards. "For the 13th year in a row, gift cards remain the most popular items on wish lists, requested by 59 percent of those surveyed," reports the National Retail Federation,[1] so I'm guessing you are one of them. If you are anything like me, you have some gift cards sitting around that have not been used. Instead of spending on entertainment this year, what if you and your spouse or kids challenged yourselves to get as much bang for your gift card buck as possible. If you have a Target gift card, instead of buying a cute necklace, what if you purchased the game Codenames (our family's favorite) and played that on Friday nights with homemade pizza instead of going out to dinner and a movie? Or use that Starbucks gift card to buy a pound of coffee instead of three cups of coffee to go.

Earn-fifty-dollars ideas:

- We recently started renting our house on Airbnb and Vrbo while we are not in it. (I travel for work, and we visit relatives pretty regularly.) This has been a great source of additional income for us. You don't need to rent out your entire place, either. If you have a spare

---

1. "Holiday Shoppers Plan to Spend 4 Percent More This Year," NRF, October 4, 2019, https://nrf.com/media-center/press-releases/holiday-shoppers-plan-spend-4-percent-more-year.

room and like to meet interesting people, this is a great way to make some fast cash.

- Get a side hustle. If you are serious about paying down debt and increasing your emergency fund, getting a side job, even temporarily, will help you accomplish your goal more quickly. It could be something ready-made like becoming a Lyft driver, or something you create yourself. I have one friend who prepares a second meal for their neighbor each night, who in turn pays for the ingredients of both meals and a little extra for her time and effort. My friend loves to cook, so this is a win-win for everyone.

- What can you sell? Part of being ready for anything is getting rid of stuff that takes time and energy to care for, so why not make some money for your emergency fund while you declutter? I've found the Nextdoor app to be a great place to buy, sell, or just give stuff away. And since it's local, there's no boxing up and shipping your items. Just one hint: people are looking for bargains. This isn't about recouping what you spent on an item—it's about getting you one step closer to your financial goals.

Once you know where you stand financially—and where you want to be—you feel empowered to make big or small, yet significant, steps to take control of your finances and your life.

YOUR PLAN

Set a date to assess your finances. Write your next steps in your Ready for Anything notebook with the goals in this chapter in mind.

Don't forget to set deadlines. Remember, this is a marathon, not a sprint. Even if something unexpected happens, readjust your timeline and keep working toward living debt-free and having three months of savings.

Include this checklist in your notebook and check them off as you go:

Goal date:

1. Save up 100 one-dollar bills (if you haven't already). _____

2. Pay off consumable debts. _____

3. Build a buffer fund of $1,000. _____

CHAPTER NINE

PREP #6: CREATE AN EMERGENCY FUND

Being an optimist, I've finally realized that I've lived my whole life backward.

I would roll along merrily in life, buying what I needed (and sometimes wanted) when I needed it and when I wanted it.

And then I would be completely, 100 percent in shock when I hit a bump in my life. The dog needed to go to the vet. I had a fender bender in the grocery store parking lot. And I would have to scramble to cover the expense. Borrowing cash, using a credit card, and panicking were my three go-to moves.

The final straw when I knew I had to make a change in my life was the day I proudly came home from work and showed my mom my brand-new leather boots that cost over three hundred dollars. I told her it was okay because I got them with my employee discount (I saved a whole sixty dollars!). And in the same moment I was greeted with the news that my car had been repossessed by the original owner because I hadn't been making car payments.

So yeah. Let's say that money management was not one of my strengths.

Can I tell you? This is not an awesome way to live. It is incredibly hard to live at the mercy of anything that can go wrong at any time. Having a sore tooth, a broken taillight, or a death screen on the computer take you out financially is beyond painful.

And here is what I've discovered about those small expenses: when you don't have the money to pay them as they happen, they don't magically go away. (I'm sure you figured this out much earlier than I did.) And when you don't pay your car registration on time (which, technically, isn't a surprise bill but always felt like a surprise to me), not only do you still have to pay the actual bill but also the late fees that go along with it. And then there was the time I got pulled over for expired tags and had a fine that was double what the registration was, and . . . Well, let's just say that having a buffer so you can pay expenses when they come in and not six months later when court fees are being threatened is a great idea.

START WITH A BUFFER

Eventually the goal is to have enough money saved to replace three months' worth of expenses. But start with a smaller goal. The buffer fund is $1,000. This fund's entire purpose is to make sure you don't have to use a credit card or go into debt when the next minor (or kind of major) problem arises. When the dishwasher decides that cleaning dishes just isn't fun anymore, when your cat decides to eat a rubber band, requiring surgery and the cone of shame, or your car decides to take up smoking, you don't have to panic, because you have your buffer fund to take care of it. Instead of charging it to your credit card and having to pay it off with interest, you can now take care of the urgent situation without panic and without paying anyone interest. The only one you are paying back is you. This buffer also gets you into the habit of paying yourself first instead of playing catch-up after every small crisis.

I have found that the best way to make these financial sprints happen is to set small doable goals. Work with others in your family, or if you are doing this on your own, work with someone else who will brainstorm with you ways to meet your goals, hold you accountable, and celebrate with you along the way as you achieve your goals.

If you don't magically have $1,000 lying around to create your buffer, don't panic. Hopefully you have your 100 one-dollar bills. Those, my friend, are already 10 percent of your buffer fund. Now set a goal and figure out how you will get your next one hundred dollars.

What do you do if you have a crisis and you don't have your emergency fund built up yet? Say your dryer has decided "Nah" and you have only $200 saved up. It's time to make some choices:

1. See if you can postpone spending any money until you can save up and pay cash for the repair or the new dryer.
    - I have kept appliances limping along by googling "How to repair a Samsung (model number) dishwasher" or "Samsung dishwasher error code: _____" and watched YouTube tutorials on how to fix small issues. Then I fixed the appliance myself.
    - When our dryer died, we spent about four months without it by hanging all our clothes to dry. I bought

a basic clothes rack and put it in our bathtub (during the winter) and dried our clothes on that and on hangers while we saved up for a new dryer. Now, during the spring, summer, and fall, I don't even use a dryer much of the time since nature is able to do the drying for me.

○ We had one friend who didn't have a washer and dryer. She offered to come cook us dinner in exchange for using our washer and dryer on a day we wouldn't be using ours. Genius. I bought the dinner ingredients, she got clean clothes, and we got Chicken Kiev. It was a win-win for everyone.

2. See if you can pay less money.

○ Is it possible to have the item repaired, or is it dead? I like to do my research online before calling in a repair person for an appliance. There is nothing worse than spending one hundred dollars on a repair guy to come out only to tell you, "Yep, it would cost more to fix it than to buy another one." But if a repair can get another couple of years out of your investment, it's well worth making that happen.

○ On sale: If you can use some of the techniques in the section on postponing spending above, you may be able to wait it out and get a great sale on the item you need to replace. Recently we needed to replace both our washer and dryer. (Don't you love when drama comes in twos?) Because we could make our old set limp along for another few weeks, we were able to wait until we found a sale on a high-capacity washer and dryer. We got exactly what we wanted, they threw in free delivery (to our mountain house, which is no small deal), and we paid less than we'd expected.

- ○ Compromise on the small stuff. The washer and dryer set we purchased was already on sale. The floor models we looked at were gunmetal gray—very nice looking. But after we made friends with the sales associate, Daisy, she let us in on what should not be a secret but apparently is: if we bought the exact same models in white, we would save $200 on each appliance. Since we were replacing white appliances, we decided that we loved white appliances. *Boom!* We saved $400 total.

3. See if you can find a temporary solution.

Sometimes you just need something to get by until you can afford what you know you really need to get the job done.

- ○ Ask around. I've had great luck posting on Facebook about things we were looking to buy. We have a great network of people, and they know other people who are moving or remodeling, or are just serial upgraders who always want the latest and greatest. One of our friends is a real estate agent, and when she found out we needed a slow cooker, she donated one from a house she was asked to clean out and sell. The family said she could personally keep or sell all the contents of the home.
- ○ Look on Craigslist or the Nextdoor app for cheap "get by" appliances until you can afford what you want.

BE SOMEONE ELSE'S SOLUTION

The other side of this financial equation? You can be the temporary solution for someone else.

Not only is this a great way to live more Christlike, but it builds great community. And great community is important in many areas of our lives. It also has many tangible and intangible benefits when it comes to being prepared.

Be the first on Facebook to say, "Come to my house, watch my Netflix, and use my washer and dryer!" Take people a meal; loan them your Weedwacker. Be the kind of neighbor you want to live next door to.

As a work-at-home writer with kids who have their own modes of transportation, I used my minivan infrequently. Sure, I made occasional trips to Target or ran errands, but it wasn't as if I was depending on my car to make an income or transport other humans around. So when people had car trouble, we were able to loan them our van. Sure, that meant that I sometimes ran errands in the evening, but that wasn't a big deal.

Let's be clear: if you wanted to borrow this minivan, you must have been desperate. It was fifteen years old, had survived my kids' childhoods, had survived transporting those kids as teenagers, and had survived each of those teenagers learning to drive. The seats were wonky, and the radio/CD player didn't work. (I'll just laugh if you ask about Bluetooth.) And I'm grateful that the interior color was Desert Sand, which happens to be the same color as cola and coffee spills. Ask me how I know. But if you had a job that relied on you actually showing up, the minivan could get you there.

You have assets in your life that could help people. Maybe

it's the ability to babysit a child after school for an hour until the child's dad gets off work. Maybe your kitchen is functional and you could double up on your dinner for a week while your friend's kitchen is out of order. Always be thinking about how you could be the buffer in someone else's life. Nothing brings people together more than helping one another through a crisis. Be the body of Christ with others.

WHEN THE INEVITABLE FINANCIAL EMERGENCY STRIKES

Your buffer fund is there to be used. If you have an emergency, use your buffer! But your next step is to replace your emergency savings as quickly as possible.

Whenever that buffer is under $1,000, this is the time to forgo movies, pack a brown bag, eat from the bottom of your freezer, and use coupons. Do everything you can to save money so that you are ready for the next unexpected crisis. (But you're smart, because you are expecting the unexpected crisis. Clever you!) Remember, the eventual goal is to have enough money saved to cover three months' worth of expenses.

Say that your current monthly expenses are $3,000. If you lost your job, you would need $9,000 saved to live at the same level you are living at now.

Can we all agree that $9,000 is an overwhelming amount of money to be putting aside for a rainy day?

But my readers are smart. You know that if you have a sudden job loss, a major medical bill, or some other financial disaster, life will not just keep going along the same as it did before. So before you throw up your hands and say that you can never save for three months' worth of expenses, figure out exactly how much you need to save to survive three months without income.

Think through all the expenses you would eliminate if you experienced a financial crisis:

- eating out
- cable or satellite
- vacations
- gift buying
- home improvements
- clothing
- entertainment (having people over as well as going out)
- putting money into savings
- large purchases you are saving for

And some of your expenses would be greatly reduced:

- gas
- tithe (If your income decreases drastically, so does your tithe. Simple as that.)
- charitable giving
- groceries (Not only would you be eating into your two-week supply, but you would also be buying different foods than the foods you would purchase if you had a steady income.)

So the first thing you need to do is figure out what you actually need to live on for three months with a drastically reduced lifestyle. Think about your current expenses, and then deduct from those any expenses that you could live without for three months.

Also think through some temporary resources you might avail yourself of during a time of crisis. Is there a food bank you could visit during a financial crisis? Does your local church have resources that could help you navigate a difficult time?

This is not the time to let pride get in your way. When I was a single mom going through a divorce, my kids qualified for free lunches through the school district. Yes, I could have packed them a lunch every day, but not only did this save me money during the roughest time of my life, it was also two fewer things I had to be concerned with as I was working full-time and taking care of two junior high school students. There are programs in place to help families during difficult times. I didn't have any other government assistance (and hadn't before or since), but I am grateful to this day for this help during a very difficult time.

When you have determined your bottom-line figure, set up a savings account goal. The good news is that you're already familiar with various ways to save and earn extra money. So save just as you did for your $1,000 buffer fund—one hundred dollars at a time.

YOUR PLAN

Figure out your bare minimum monthly expenses for if you or your spouse lost your income. Multiply that by three. This is your goal for your emergency fund.

Write this figure and your plan for saving it in your notebook. Make sure you write down your goal date.

chapter TEN

PREP #7:
STORE TWO WEEKS'
WORTH OF FOOD

Last night Roger and I woke up to an earthshaking *Crackkk* outside our house and contemplated the end of the world until we experienced the eerie silence that comes after your heart stops pounding in your ears.

With California's drought conditions for the past five years, our trees' roots are not very stable. A rainstorm with high winds had brought down a giant tree.

Fortunately, it just missed our neighbor's house.

And then later, because of the downed tree's location, our power company had to shut off power to almost everyone in our neighborhood for several hours to deal with the tree. It's good to know we have what we need inside our house to be safe and comfortable for the days to come.

Part of what we all need in case of emergency is a small (or not so small) stockpile of food and water. In this chapter we will concentrate on food.

Most preppers will tell you to have at least a year's worth of food on hand, and some hard-core preppers will let you know that if you have anything less than thirty years' worth of food stored up, you are doomed.

We are not hard-core preppers. Yes, my goal is to have more than two weeks' worth of food ready, especially because we have a house in the mountains where the closest real grocery store is thirty minutes away. By putting up two weeks' worth of food, you give yourself more choices in an emergency situation or a job loss. Those are two weeks when you don't have to worry about what you're going to eat. It also gives you some time to make decisions about what you will do to keep going.

HARD-CORE PREPPING VS. READY FOR ANYTHING

Looking through prepping websites and books, you may be convinced that to be prepared you need to order thousands of dollars' worth of food in specially sealed tubs. And depending on your circumstances, you may want to consider long-term storage for your food. For example, do you live somewhere without good infrastructure? Do you work seasonally, so the potential for being out of work is greater than average?

For most of us, the right place to start is with two weeks of nonperishable food that can be purchased at the grocery store. This is a great way to start for a couple of reasons:

1. It's inexpensive. Stocking while you're already at the store makes a lot of sense financially. When you see

a sale on canned peaches (which you already use and your family loves), you can buy a few more than your family will use that week.

I watch for sales through my store's app and in the weekly flyer that comes in the mail. I plan to use a small portion of my weekly food budget toward my stockpile.

2. You can also buy in bulk. The next time you're at Costco or Sam's Club and you hesitate to buy the flat of canned corn when you consider how long it will take you to use it, buy it anyway. Half of it can go into your pantry to be used over the next month or two, and the other half can go into your stockpile for an emergency.

3. Buying a bunch of prepackaged food you can store long term is convenient, but what do you do when you are in an emergency and your four-year-old won't eat the freeze-dried scrambled eggs? That is the last thing you want to worry about in a natural disaster. Instead, you want to have some family favorites, and even a few comfort foods in the midst of an emergency, especially if you are going to be in your home for an extended amount of time.

4. Ingredients give you options. With ready-made meals, you get what you get. In an extreme emergency, where you have to leave your home, you will be grateful for those ready-to-eat meals to which you just add water and heat. But for situations when you're at home, such as long-term power outages or job loss, you will be grateful for the different combinations of meals you can create by not having meals on hand, but ingredients instead.

Canned peaches can be used as a side for a sandwich at lunch. But they can also be made into a cobbler with just a few ingredients. Canned peaches can also be reduced into the most heavenly syrup for pancakes and waffles, or even pan fried with pork chops for an amazing dinner.

5. Real food keeps things normal when the rest of life is hard. Having a two-week supply of foods that you already eat can make life seem a little more consistent when a family situation, job loss, or other emergency throws you off balance. If these items are part of your normal day-to-day existence, it is easy to prepare meals that you've already prepared dozens of times without having to learn new skills.

PANTRY INVENTORY

Is your pantry where things go to die?

One of the mistakes I've seen people who want to be prepared make is going out and buying all the canned and dried food known to man and then sitting back and waiting for the "big one" (whatever that is) to hit, secure in the notion that they have canned peaches to last them until Taylor Swift starts having farewell tours. They see no need for a plan; they will get organized and figure out how to put meals together when the disaster hits.

I don't want you to get caught with only forty-seven cans of peaches and no protein when disaster strikes. Being ready for anything means we're a little smarter with how we stock our pantry.

1. Don't spend money needlessly.

   One of the ways to be ready for anything is not to spend money for food you already have or food that no one in your family will eat. Instead, discover what you already have (and you and your family already love to eat) and work from there.

2. Plan now so you don't have to make decisions when you're already overwhelmed.

   In the midst of a local or family crisis is not the time to try to pull together a can of peaches, some ramen noodles, and Spam and try to make a dinner your family will eat. The time to plan is now, when there is no crisis, and then make sure you have the right stuff on hand to execute your plan.

3. Get organized now so you can always know what you have.

   Again, the time to get organized is not when disaster hits. One of the best ways to feel powerful and in control when it comes to your food supply is to know what you have and store it in an organized way.

Have a Cupboard Cleanout

Don't be one of those people who has a vague notion that because there is so much in your cupboards, surely, if a disaster hit, you would have plenty to eat.

What if those cupboards contained a bunch of flour and rice, a ton of canned fruit, several expired boxes of pancake mix, and those six boxes of cake mix you bought on sale before you realized no one in your family likes carrot cake?

While I don't advocate throwing out food you will eat, it is not a good idea to keep those foods no one will eat "just in case." It's like adding an imaginary $1,000 to your bank account. It may feel better in your head, but all it's doing is giving you a false sense of security. Trust me, the last thing you want in a panic situation is to try to force your family to eat beets when they've never tried them or have declared their hatred of them.

When people ask me which of my books they should read first, *Clutter Free* or *Organized for Life*, I press *Clutter Free* into their hands and say, "You can't organize clutter."

So the first thing you should do is declutter your food. Go through all the food in your house. (This could be done over a few days if you have a lot.) It is time to throw it away or, if the package is unopened and not expired, donate it to a friend, family member, or food bank.

We all have nonsense lurking in our cabinets, like leftover dried fruit from a gift basket we were given or a can of sardines from when our dad was in town. Get rid of as much as you can, right now, to make room for your new, organized, ready-for-anything life.

The bonus? Getting your cupboards all cleaned out will make your everyday meal prep so much easier. Trust me. You will be sending me gift cards as thank-yous every time you make dinner.

Take an Inventory

Now that you're all cleaned out and organized, it's time to determine what you actually have on hand. On our website, www.kathilipp.com/rfa, I have a food inventory sheet. Download that and get an accurate assessment of what food you actually have, and determine what you need to buy to make complete meals.

Date Everything

Once you have everything in your fridge, freezer, and pantry that you want to keep, do yourself a favor and use a bold marker to write the expiration date on it, and put the date on your inventory sheet. This way you will know what to use up first so you won't be throwing away food because it is out of date.

Plan from Your Pantry

When we move into the next chapter and start planning your two-week stash of food, make sure you have your inventory sheet ready so you can get inspired for all your meals.

One of the hardest things to do is to try and plan meals out of air. But when you look at your inventory and see that you have canned tomatoes, corn, taco seasoning, and chicken, suddenly the need to find a chicken tortilla soup recipe becomes urgent, and not only are you planning, but you're excited to be planning. (Plus you have the thrill of knowing that all those cans are not just ready for an emergency but also ready to feed you day to day.)

One of the things this exercise did for me was to help me get excited about cooking again. As we all know, cooking for our families, our spouses, or just ourselves can become pretty monotonous. But this MacGyver cooking—where you take what you have and make something amazing out of it—gets really interesting. It makes me feel smart and creative that I am making delicious (or at least adventurous) meals out of things that were sitting unused in my pantry.

WHAT TO STOCK UP ON

What you stock in your pantry is a little basic common sense mixed with personal taste. One of the biggest mistakes I see people make is buying foods just because they're on sale—that their family wouldn't normally eat. They assume their family will eat anything if they're hungry enough. But even if you are almost completely out of food, if tuna makes your stomach turn on a normal day, you are not magically going to want to eat it during an emergency or when you're broke.

So as you do your pantry planning and stockpiling, try to purchase foods your family normally eats. This may mean different versions of food (canned chicken instead of frozen chicken breasts), but the usual foods will offer comfort during an uncomfortable time.

Plus, even shelf-stable foods expire. If you buy things that your family normally eats, you can rotate the food regularly, based on expiration dates, which ensures that you won't end up with an emergency supply that is uneaten and expired.

CANNED/DRIED MEATS: canned chicken, tuna, salmon, Spam

CANNED SOUPS: just-add-water soups, stews, and chili

CANNED FRUITS: peaches, pears, mandarin oranges, fruit cocktail

CANNED VEGETABLES: green beans, mushrooms, carrots, pickles, tomatoes, tomato paste, tomato sauce, stewed tomatoes, peas, mixed veggies, corn

DRIED FRUITS: apples, mango, pineapple, blueberries, strawberries, apricots, raisins, prunes

GRAINS: rice, oatmeal, pasta, cereal

CANNED BEANS: garbanzo, pinto, black, kidney, edamame

SEASONINGS: a basic spice rack with savory and sweet spices. Also salt and pepper.

BAKING ITEMS: flour, sugar, baking powder, baking soda, yeast

MILK: powdered, canned, shelf-stable, sweetened condensed, evaporated

BEVERAGES: coffee, tea, hot chocolate mix, powdered drink mixes, bottled juice, drinks with electrolytes (Gatorade, etc.)

OTHER STAPLES: salsa, broth, onions, garlic

PREPARATION METHODS

When thinking through your two-week supply, you'll also need to make sure that you have ways to prep your food. You can't buy a bunch of microwave meals and call it a day.

We have a couple of different options when it comes to off-grid food prep. We have a grill to barbecue meats. We can make oatmeal by putting a pot of water on to boil. We also have a small camp stove we can use to heat a can of soup or some canned sausages. We have plenty of fuel for each of these cooking methods to get us through two weeks.

If you don't already have a barbecue or camp stove, your best bet is to pick up a small hibachi grill and a few bags of charcoal so you will be able to heat up meals if the power goes out. You'll also want to plan the location of these cooking devices. Obviously, because of carbon monoxide poisoning, you can't use them indoors. Can you set it up on a covered deck or other secure place if the weather is bad?

If you have the funds, another option is to pick up a small generator for a quick cooking job on a hot plate or electric frying pan. A small generator can run you as little as $100 (make sure you have a generous supply of gas or propane).

PREPPING YOUR STORAGE

When you think of food storage, you may think about those TLC shows about extreme couponers and their bunkers filled with shelves jam-packed with seven hundred boxes of mac and cheese bought for a penny each on sale with a double coupon and a rebate.

Let's be clear: that is not what my food storage looks like.

One of my friends was moving to Arkansas thirteen years ago and was giving away three small bookcases. The bookshelves became my starter pantry for storing canned foods. These are not big shelves, but because they are small, I know everything I have stored there. Also, because they are small, I rotate through my food pretty quickly so very few items expire or go to waste.

My suggestions for food storage:

1. **Have one spot for each item.** In other words, do not store the canned garbanzo beans behind the kidney beans. You need to know what you have, and the best way to do that is to be able to see what's on the shelves.
2. **Keep a running inventory.** My inventory sheet is less for seeing what I have on hand and more for figuring out what I need to buy at the store. I have a minimum of how much I want on hand for each item (e.g., three cans of pinto beans and six cans of chicken or meats), and if it looks like I will run below that, I will put it on my list for the next time I'm at wherever I usually buy that particular item.
3. **Use a green sticker.** I put a green sticker on anything I need to use up. If that soup is about to expire or the

cracker box is open and it's time to eat them up, I put a green sticker on the container, saying, "Use me up!"

I have a roll of green stickers handy in the pantry for this exact purpose. This is so much better than discovering that something expired months ago.

4. **Make your storage work for you.** We have shelving in our garage that holds much of our day-to-day food as well as our two-week supply. (We mix our inventory because we constantly want to be eating from and replenishing our two-week supply so it's always up to date. Just because something is in a can doesn't mean it will be good forever.)

On this shelving we either store the cans on top of each other or use chrome stackable can racks. These racks tip down slightly in the front so the cans roll forward as you use them. Either way, it is easy to see what you have and to be able to keep up on your inventory system.

In the mountains, we have some furry friends who would love nothing more than to take advantage of any opportunity to eat everything that isn't in a can. So we store pasta, cereals, rice, and snacks in easy-to-access plastic tubs.

MENU PLANNING

Your two-week food stockpile is like your checking account. That money is always in motion. You use it to pay for everyday living expenses, but hopefully you never let the balance get below a set amount. Your two-week food supply works the same way.

Ninety percent of what you have gets used from day to day—you just have a thoughtful surplus to cover two weeks. Most days you will have more than two weeks' worth of food on hand, but you will always, at a minimum, have a two-week supply.

When you create a menu, you will have all the ingredients on hand to create everything on that menu. Always have those ingredients in your pantry, and never dip below a two-week supply.

For your two weeks of emergency food, plan for ingredients that don't require refrigeration or freezing (in case your power goes out) but are still part of your everyday rotation.

Here are some things to consider when creating your two-week stockpile:

1. Think Comfort

When an emergency hits, you are not going to be wanting to stay on your weight-loss diet. In a natural disaster, calories are your friend. You will want familiar food that you and your family will look forward to eating. Think about what your menu looks like now. Are there easy ways to replicate it with shelf-stable foods? We have a salad every day, but that won't be possible if we're limited to shelf-stable foods. So I plan for other ways to get the brightness of salads into our meal plan without lettuce. Canned or jarred marinated artichokes and carrots, canned garbanzo and other beans, canned and dried fruits and veggies will all help us feel like we are not missing out on our favorite lunch.

I also have a big supply of canned vegetable soups (which we tend to eat in the cooler months instead of a salad). I have a few different flavors to keep things interesting and enjoyable.

Most mornings include oatmeal and dried fruit, so that will be a pretty easy transition if we have to go off grid. As long as I have the ingredients, water (or canned or dried milk), and our camp stove, I will be set.

And when it comes to comfort, don't stop your thinking at food. Coffee first thing in the morning is my favorite way to start the day. I have at least a two-week supply of coffee at all times and a French press (very important for any coffee drinker's emergency supply kit). As long as I can heat water, I can make coffee using the French press.

2. Think Variety

The image I used to have of preppers is that they had a ten-year supply of beans and that was about all. But variety is incredibly important when it comes to your emergency stash. Not only does variety provide comfort, it also provides the nutrition humans need.

3. Think Ease

You need food that is easy to store and prepare. Emergency situations call for all kinds of other tasks to be done (like hauling water from the creek), and you may not have the energy or time to create elaborate meals.

4. Think Access

What cooking methods will you have available if all your power goes out? Will you have a solar cooker, a camp stove, a grill, a fire stove? Your cooking method will determine what kind of food you will plan for your two-week supply (and beyond).

A solar cooker is tricky for us here in Northern California. Most months it doesn't get hot enough to cook anything. And if it's raining, no matter where you are, you are out of luck. So in both the mountains and the city, we would rely on our grill and our camp stove, and also our indoor woodstove.

BUFFER STOCKPILE VS. EMERGENCY STOCKPILE

If you do a bigger stockpile, think of it as your emergency stockpile. (Similar to your emergency fund.)

My emergency stockpile is for when things really go off the rails. There's been a car accident, the dog needs surgery, one of us loses our job, or some other crisis occurs.

We need money in our checking account for day-to-day expenses and a little cushion, our buffer fund, for unexpected expenses. Then we need an emergency fund to help us be more stable in the long run. That is exactly how we should think about our two-week supply of food, our buffer stockpile, and our bigger stockpile of food, the emergency stockpile.

Many people buy fancy, expensive survivalist food to be prepared for a disaster. This is a perfectly reasonable approach if you are trying to be prepared for longer than two weeks. And many circumstances call for you to be prepared for much longer than two weeks, especially if you live in a vulnerable area. But since this book is all about getting you ready for 3-2-3, we'll concentrate on the first two weeks after a disaster hits, which will involve the use of canned and packaged foods that you already use. Once you have that down, you can move into all the freeze-dried chicken stews you want.

YOUR STOCKPILE ISN'T JUST FOR YOU

When you are thinking through what you will eat over two weeks, start with a menu that will feed everyone who lives at your house for fourteen days. Then think about the reality of your situation. Will it just be you, your spouse, and your two kids who will rely on your stockpile in an emergency situation?

We have adult kids who live in the area. While they have some emergency supplies, they have tiny Silicon Valley–size apartments where they can't store very much. Three of them could get here on foot in an emergency. So guess who will be on our doorstep if an emergency happens?

Plus, we have a neighbor with whom we share our lives. We would want to do our best to be a good neighbor to her as well. So now we are talking six people. Our two-week supply for Roger and me would translate into about a four- or five-day supply for the six of us. So our two-week supply is a great start, but we will need to triple it if there will be six of us.

Think about what a two-week supply would be for everyone in your house, and then think about who would likely show up on your doorstep.

YOUR PLAN

Set a date with your family to organize and inventory your pantry. Create a list of what you need to buy to have a two-week supply, and then make a plan for your grocery shopping (e.g., spend twenty dollars per week on surplus food for eight weeks). Make sure your plan is realistic about the number of people who can be supported for long periods of time. You only have so much storage room in your home.

Set a deadline. When do you plan to organize and take inventory?

Write down the date you'll finish stocking your two-week supply.

CHAPTER ELEVEN

PREP #8: PRACTICE CRISIS COOKING

Creating Meals from Your Two-Week Supply

I was recently talking with an acquaintance at a party, and we got on the subject of this book. He told me in no uncertain terms that he would be fine if anything went down because he had wholesale store–size boxes of cereal.

I asked him, "What are you going to use for milk?"

He had never thought of that.

Think through all your meals and see if you are relying on any fresh, fridge, or freezer products to make them happen. If so, you need to rethink your meals or come up with substitutions for those perishable items.

Here is a sample of our menu plan. It's not fancy. No one will be making Baked Alaska while the power is out at our house. But we have a basic plan for food we will eat and that we can actually prepare if a disaster occurs and we need time to figure things out.

DAY 1

BREAKFAST

Oatmeal with dried fruit

Coffee with individual creamers

LUNCH

Tuna salad

Crackers

Canned pears

DINNER

Pantry chili

Cast iron corn bread

DAY 2

BREAKFAST

Leftover corn bread with canned sausages

Canned peaches

Coffee with individual creamers

LUNCH

Rice and beans

Canned vegetables

DINNER

Canned chicken and veggie soup

Cast iron buttermilk biscuits

DAY 3

BREAKFAST

Pancakes with poached peaches

LUNCH

Leftover buttermilk biscuits

Peanut butter and jam

Canned pineapple

DINNER

Satay soba noodles with canned salmon

SHOPPING FOR YOUR STASH

To-Go Packets

One of the items I've added to my stash is a bundle of to-go packets of mustard, mayo, ketchup, and relish. (You can order these online from Amazon. I am in no way suggesting that you load up the next time you go to your favorite fast-food joint.) These are great for packed lunches and travel, but, also, in a power outage situation, I can have some mayo and relish with my tuna salad without opening a whole jar that will just spoil.

I also like individual creamers (the kind that don't require refrigeration). I use them when I travel (stored in a travel soap case), so even if I'm stuck with hotel coffee, I'm not stuck with powdered creamer.

I also have on hand a variety pack of individual salad dressings. I use these to pack in my husband's lunch and take when I travel, but in case of emergency, I can use the dressing packets to add some variety to meals we are creating with shelf-stable and canned foods.

The next time you have food delivered and you get too many soy sauce packets, don't pitch them; add them to your two-week stash as a flavor bump.

Spices and Seasonings

Many of the meals you create will have the same base: things like chicken, tuna, salmon, rice, canned veggies, and canned fruit. Where you can kick up the variety is in the spices and seasonings you use.

We have a great set of spices that we have amassed for different flavor profiles. Chicken and rice with water chestnuts and canned veggies, along with some five-spice powder, give you a great-tasting Asian meal. Chicken and rice with stewed tomatoes and thyme, oregano, and garlic make for a delicious Italian flavor profile.

These recipes also work if the disaster is financial and we still have power and water at our house but immediately need to stop buying groceries and divert our money into other places.

Long-Lasting Fresh Foods

A few fresh items you can have on hand that will last a few weeks include those in the following chart. All should be stored in a cool, dry, dark spot.

Garlic	A few weeks to a few months
Onions	Whole, 3 to 4 weeks
Potatoes (new)	1 week

Potatoes (baking)	Up to 2 months stored in a brown paper bag
Pumpkin	Up to 1 month
Squash (winter), whole	Up to 1 month
Sweet potatoes	Up to 1 month

GET CREATIVE IN THE KITCHEN

Much of what I'm going to suggest in this section will help you during your noncrisis times as well. We all are looking for ways to save money, time, and energy when it comes to feeding ourselves and our families.

One of the best ways that you can get ready for anything with your food supply is to start cooking creatively.

Stop Being a Slave to Your Recipes

Your recipe calls for granulated garlic and you don't have any in the house, so you start searching the internet for something else to eat tonight. No need.

I'm guessing you could replace that granulated garlic with either fresh or pureed garlic. Or leave it out entirely and bulk up the white onions. Unless you're baking something, most recipes do not live or die on one ingredient.

If you want to try a recipe but don't have all the ingredients, figure out if an ingredient can be replaced by something else or left out altogether. I've found that in many recipes a meat can be substituted for another meat, a veggie for a veggie, and a spice for a similar spice.

If you don't have half the ingredients, it's probably time to try something different. But if it's just one or two, figure out a way to make them work.

Think of What You Have, Not What You Need

Most people plan their meals backward. They start by thinking of what they want to eat and then buy the ingredients for that meal. But the more efficient and economical way of planning your meals is to see what you already have and then base your dinner or meal plan off that.

This will help you so much if you ever need to "eat off the fat of the land" (i.e., not go to the store for a while so that you can save money or don't have access to a store).

LOOP Meals

LOOP Meals (or leftovers on purpose) are when you purposely make too much of a meal (often a main dish or meat) so that you will have leftovers on purpose for a following meal.

During an emergency situation, you will not want to cook rice multiple times a day. Instead, cook rice once in the morning and use it for lunch mixed in with chicken and veggies, and then for dinner for rice, beans, and veggies with seasoning.

Also think ahead about whether you need, for example, some shredded carrot tomorrow for salad. If you will be putting carrots in your stew tonight, go ahead and prep all the carrots you need for both meals now.

Perform Leftover Magic

Sometimes you plan for leftovers (like LOOP meals), and sometimes leftovers just happen. Last night we had friends over for grilled steak. While we knew there might be leftovers, we were actually pretty surprised that two full steaks remained after everyone left. We underestimated just how big those steaks were!

So this morning I brainstormed all the things we could do with leftover steak:

Steak fajitas with grilled veggies and beans

Steak tacos (shredding the beef and adding that and fresh veggies to a taco shell)

Steak and potato soup (adding some leftover veggies and potatoes to the meat and pouring in beef broth)

Steak and pasta (instead of pasta and meatballs, adding strips of steak to pasta and marinara)

Baked potatoes (add all the fixings and top with shredded beef)

Steak salad (buying a salad kit and adding strips of steak as a topping)

In the end, I decided on steak and potato soup since we've had a lot of warm days in a row and today there is a chill in the air.

If you experience a power outage, keeping leftovers for long may be impossible. That is why it is important to get creative with any and all food so that absolutely nothing goes to waste.

PLAN YOUR MEALS DURING THE NONCRISIS DAYS

The best time to plan your meals is when there is no crisis. Practice every week planning meals for your family. In the midst of planning those meals for which you have the luxury of fresh ingredients, make one meal a week for which you are using only pantry, shelf-stable items. Practice making soup from canned broth and dried pasta, canned veggies and chicken, dehydrated mushrooms and onions, and you will be ready for the day when you need to make a meal without the benefit of your fridge.

One meal a week made from shelf-stable ingredients will go a long way to lessen your anxiety when a crisis comes. You will be able to approach your pantry with confidence because you've made these meals before.

FRESH FIRST!

"Fresh first!" is a motto Roger and I have when we're meal planning. If I'm coming up with the week's menus and I am trying to decide what food we will have on what day, part of my deciding factor is "Fresh first!" In other words, if I have the choice of prepping the fresh chicken I bought at the store this week or pulling out frozen chicken breasts for dinner, I prep the fresh chicken. If I'm deciding between leftovers from last night's dinner for lunch or making a peanut butter and jelly sandwich, I'm going for leftovers. This also ensures that I'm not just taking fruits and vegetables on a road trip to my fridge before sending them to the great composting bin in the sky.

In case of a power outage, you'll want to use up the perishable food first before cooking with shelf-stable foods. You'll have about two days before freezer food thaws, so you'll want to put that in the rotation early as well.

THE FOOD OF LEAST RESISTANCE

Most of us tend to go with the food of least resistance. We skip over the chicken breasts that need to be cooked and the broccoli that needs to be washed and blanched, and head right to the Cup O' Noodles that just need some hot water added (and even that can feel like a lot on some days). That is why predeciding what foods you are going to eat—and in what order—will cut down on food waste in emergency situations, as well as on the days when you just want to get dinner on the table.

Practice "fresh first" every day so that when a disaster hits, it is your first instinct. You will use up everything fresh first so that you can save your shelf-stable food for later on.

TWO-WEEK STOCKPILE RECIPE IDEAS

Whether it's a job loss, power loss, or some other emergency, you'll want some recipes on hand to plan your emergency menus. The next two pages provide some ideas to get you started.

YOUR PLAN

Write out the menus you would use if you only had access to shelf-stable foods. Make sure to include only recipes using ingredients you have stocked in your pantry. Make a copy of the menus and recipes to keep in your emergency binder. (We're going to put that together in the next chapter, so keep your copies handy.)

SPANISH RICE

10 minutes hands-on prep
Ready in 30 minutes

Ingredients

2 tablespoons oil

2 tablespoons chopped onion

1 1/2 cups uncooked white or brown rice

2 cups chicken broth

1 cup chunky salsa

Directions

1. Heat oil in a large skillet over medium heat.
2. Stir in onion and cook until tender, about 5 minutes.
3. Add rice to skillet, stirring often.
4. When rice begins to brown, stir in chicken broth and salsa.
5. Reduce heat, cover, and simmer 20 minutes, until liquid has been absorbed by the rice.

NOTE: Cast iron skillets are perfect for any heat source, whether it's a stovetop, a barbecue grill, or a camp stove.

Other Ideas:

Add a can of chicken to create a main dish. Add it at the last minute just to heat it through.

Substitute chopped up Italian stewed tomatoes for the salsa and sausages for a different flavor profile.

KATHI'S CHILI

A less-spicy version that even kids will like.

Ingredients

1 16-ounce can chicken

1 cup chopped onions

1 clove garlic, minced

1 16-ounce can stewed tomatoes

1 16-ounce can kidney beans, drained

1 16-ounce can tomato sauce

1 tablespoon chili powder

1/2 teaspoon basil

1 6-ounce can tomato paste

Pepper, to taste

Directions

1. In large saucepan, cook chicken, onions, and garlic until onions are translucent and meat is brown.
2. Drain.
3. Stir in tomatoes, kidney beans, tomato sauce, tomato paste, chili powder, basil, and pepper.
4. Bring to a boil.
5. Reduce heat, cover, and simmer 30 minutes.

TWELVE

PREP #9: CREATE AN EMERGENCY BINDER

I am a binder girl.

For different projects in my life, I have different binders. Most of my life and work takes place in the digital world, but when I'm very serious about a project, I'm going to print it and put it in a binder. The sign that I'm serious? The amount of time I spend picking the perfect binder for that project.

Getting prepped is a serious project.

In an emergency, I want all my important information in one place. I want my emergency contact numbers, my recipes for pantry pasta primavera, and notes about where my batteries are located all in one place. I want a binder.

As I've thought through what I need in my emergency binder, nothing has helped me more than what I've learned as an Airbnb host. Dozens of strangers stay for two to five days at a time at our two Airbnb properties (the homes where we also alternatively live). On the Airbnb website, as well as in a binder at each house, we have all the information anyone would need to be both safe and comfortable. I've included things like emergency shutoff procedures for the gas, electricity, and water; directions on how to get out of the house from any room; and even where the can opener is located in the kitchen. Having to consider each house and how guests will find what they need when they need it has helped me think through my home when it comes to prepping.

Consider your own home and think about the instructions and information you'd leave as if you were leaving them for a complete stranger. Maybe when disaster hits you will be out of town and your spouse will be the one who needs the binder. Or maybe it's your teenage son who will be home alone.

WHY YOU NEED A BINDER

We've already established that I'm not a clearheaded thinker in an emergency. Remember, I'm the one who grabbed the dog and left the kid in the burning building.

I'm also someone who struggled with clutter for much of my life and spent hours searching for things. Even on a good day, finding the individual instructions for things can be challenging. Hoping they'll magically appear five minutes after a major earthquake? Nope!

That is why I need a binder.

You may have different issues, but we both need a binder before a crisis hits. Even if you have every detail memorized, a binder helps other members of the family know what to do in a crisis if you're not home at the time. I recommend that you keep your emergency binder and your planning notebook separate. You'll want to switch out pages of the binder when the information changes, and trying to keep both in the same binder will be confusing and messy.

Here are the materials you will need to create your binder:

three-ring binder
tabs
sheet protectors
zippered pouches
three-hole punch

TABS FOR YOUR BINDER

Listed below are some tabs you might want to consider for your binder. Of course, if you have other information that might help you or your family during an emergency, add sections for that information too.

Remember to think like someone who isn't familiar with your house. What will they need to know in an emergency? You want to take that head knowledge and put it to paper so that your brain is on the page for anyone who is at your house during an emergency:

- **Locations of shutoffs (water, gas, etc.)**
- **Use of emergency equipment (generator, etc.)**
- **Emergency contacts**

    Think of every number you might need to call in an emergency (or in the days following a crisis), and list them so that your spouse, older kids, or babysitter will know who to call. If you also have them in your phone, great. If you have a power outage, make sure you have a way to charge your phone so you have access to those phone numbers. Solar phone chargers are available almost anywhere you can buy other phone accessories.

- **Evacuation checklist**

    Yes, you have your bug-out bag ready to go, but if you have a little more time before you need to get out of the house, consider what else you would like to take with you and list those items. This is the list of things to grab when leaving your house for an indeterminate amount of time.

- **Disaster plan for your most likely disasters**

    In chapter 16 you'll go over your emergency plan with your family. Include that plan on a page in the binder. You'll review that plan once a year, so you'll need to update this section of the binder as your plans change.

- **Maps**

    Maps? How quaint, right? But if your internet is down or cell service is down, having a map of your area with evacuation routes marked (or the route to the home of someone you will be staying with in an emergency) can save a lot of confusion in a desperate situation.

- **Copies of important documents**

    Imagine you are in the middle of a disaster and have to spend a week in a shelter. While you are there, emergency government services are provided, but your ID is required. If you have copies of all your important documents, you are much more likely to get the services you need. Here's a list of important documents you may want to keep in your binder:

- ○ **Identification papers**
  - ▪ Government-issued IDs
  - ▪ Passports
  - ▪ Social Security cards
- ○ **Medical documents**
  - ▪ Medical records
  - ▪ Copies of medical ID cards
  - ▪ Vet records
  - ▪ Prescriptions for medicines
  - ▪ Prescriptions for eyeglasses
  - ▪ Allergies
- ○ **Legal documents**
  - ▪ Marriage certificate
  - ▪ Divorce papers
  - ▪ Homeowners, life, and health insurance policy information
  - ▪ Wills, trusts, and power of attorney documents
  - ▪ Military documents
- **Meal plan**
- **Written water plan**
- **Homeowners or rental insurance information, and insurance agency contact information**
- **Rental information**

  If you're renting your home or condo, include landlord/homeowners' association phone numbers and other important details in case you need to reach the owner of the property. If you have belongings in storage, that location and phone number would be handy here too.

- **Map of the house with current occupants' names in their respective rooms**

- **Extra sets of keys in a zippered pouch**
- **Bank information**

Not only will having all this information in one place help you in an emergency, but having it together any day will make your life easier to manage.

Keep your binder close to where you store your bug-out bags. If you need to evacuate for any reason, be sure to take the binder with you.

YOUR PLAN

Make a plan for creating your binder. Do you already have the supplies listed? If not, put them on the list for the next time you go to the office supply store.

Write down the due date for completing the binder in your Ready for Anything notebook.

THIRTEEN

PREP #10: MAKE A WATER PLAN

If there is one thing I've learned in the past six months, it is how much I've taken for granted that if I turn a knob, water will come out of the faucet. Mountain living has taught me that you can't take for granted the luxury of running water (and yes, I now consider water coming out of a faucet a "luxury"). Furthermore, you have to have a plan B (or, often in our case, a plan H) to prepare for the days you need to impersonate Laura Ingalls and figure out where your water is going to come from.

First, during the Snowmaggedon we experienced this year, even with all the precautions we'd taken, our pipes froze. So not only were we digging through four feet of frozen water (a.k.a. snow), we were out of water in the house. Oh, I just love irony. When it's happening to other people.

We had plenty of drinking water because we had prepped. But we needed water to do some fancy things like, you know, flush toilets (like I said—fancy). So my job, while Roger was digging paths in the snow and freeing our buried car, was to boil snow in pots set on top of our woodstove. Then I dumped the water into five-gallon buckets and put those buckets next to the toilets in the house for the next time they were needed.

Then, just a month later, while we were hosting a retreat at our house, the water went out again. (One of our guests was wondering why we had a tiny lake on our lawn. Turns out that lake was created by a pipe that burst. Super fun!)

This time there was no snow available for melting, but we have a seasonal creek on our property, so Roger and one of my team members, Tiffany, went out with a machete and hacked a rough trail to the creek to get us water so everyone could flush.

Like I said, you never realize how much you enjoy the luxury of flushing until you can't just hit a lever.

When we are in our "city house" we don't have the "gift" of snow to melt or a creek to collect water from, so it's important that we have what we need on hand in case of emergency. The Centers for Disease Control recommends keeping on hand one gallon of drinkable water per day for a minimum of three days for every person in your house in case of emergency.[1] But we, my friends, are ready for anything. So we are going to store a two-week water supply. If Roger and I were prepping for the two of us, for example, we would need twenty-eight gallons of water.

Remember, dogs are people too. (Okay, I know they're not, but don't tell Jake the puggle that.) And while Jake loves to drink slightly icky rainwater that has gathered on our back patio and is fine afterward, in an emergency situation, I want Jake (and Ashley the cat) to have the same quality of drinking water that Roger and I have.

---

1. "Creating & Storing an Emergency Water Supply," Centers for Disease Control, accessed October 11, 2019, www.cdc.gov/healthywater/emergency/drinking/creating-storing-emergency-water-supply.html.

In addition to our twenty-eight gallons, we also need to consider the amount of water our cat and dog will need. The CDC website says to allow for one gallon per day per pet. Use your common sense here. (My twelve-pound Russian Blue cat, Ashley, drinks less than one cup of water a day, so I'll pack accordingly.)

In that gallon of water per day per person, the CDC's recommendation is that half of it be reserved for drinking and half for hygiene.

OUR PLAN FOR WATER STORAGE

If you read traditional prepper books, you may get freaked out by the elaborate water storage systems and processes they recommend. There is no reason to lose your mind when you are preparing for a two-week supply. Promise.

1. Drinking Water

I want half of my water storage to be for drinking. And that is why we store good old-fashioned water bottles. Some extremists will tell you that storing drinking water in regular plastic bottles could cause problems, but in actuality, the Food and Drug Administration does not require an expiration date on bottled water. If manufactured and stored properly, bottled water can last indefinitely. For example, PCPs leaking into the water from the plastic is only a problem if the bottles are stored significantly above room temperature for long periods of time (such as in a car). To be safe and to keep your water tasty, store it at room temperature and away from direct sunlight.

So our first step to getting eighteen gallons of drinking water is to buy five flats of bottled water. With forty bottles each holding 16.9 ounces, that is more than five gallons of water per flat. And since we actually drink that water in non-emergency times, we keep extra on hand. We rotate the bottled water, using first-purchased bottles first.

We store these water bottles in our garage, on shelving, which helps them stay cool and out of direct sunlight. (I put a blanket over them to make sure no sunlight hits them.) If you don't have room in your garage, storing the bottles in a basement, under your bed, or in a closet is ideal.

Not only is bottled water easy to store, but when it's time to brush your teeth and the water is out, you will be grateful to have a highly portable bottle of water instead of having to lug a big jug around.

2. Bathing and General Use Water

Let's be clear here: the word *bathing* may be a little generous when describing our cleansing routine when the water is out. But you will need to keep clean for hygienic purposes and to feel somewhat normal, and let's face it, so that your friends and family still want to hang out with you during hard times. Your bathing water can be in a slightly less convenient container. My husband and I use water jugs (as we discussed in chapter 4) and make sure that the water is treated or changed out every six months to keep it fresh.

I also like to keep a supply of hygienic wipes on hand for touch-ups. This was a lifesaver when our water was out in the mountains. After a hike to grab wood, or before bed and first thing in the morning, grabbing a wipe and doing a quick cleanup to feel human again made going forward in my day possible. Plus, they will help you save water when times become desperate.

3. Your Tool Kit for Clean Water

Ninety-five percent of what I recommend in this book is common sense, and 5 percent is going to feel weird and counter-cultural. When it comes to safe water, here is your 5 percent:

A. WaterBOB

The WaterBOB is a giant liner (with lid) for your bathtub that can hold up to one hundred gallons of water at a time (and keep it clean). This would be especially helpful in a situation where you know that a disaster is likely to hit (hurricane, boil-water order for your city, etc.). Fill up the bladder, seal it, and dispense clean water as you need it.

B. Portable Aqua Water Purification Tablets

If you are stuck with water that is of "iffy" quality, having some water purification tablets handy is a great idea. You can buy one bottle, and the tablets will never expire if you don't open the lid. When Austin, Texas, was under a boil order for all their water, I heard of many families using these tablets to make absolutely sure that their water was suitable to drink and use for things like cooking or washing fruits and veggies. These tablets are not intended to be a long-term solution to bad drinking water, but when the choice is between water that isn't 100 percent pure and the tablets, I'll take the tablets every time.

C. LifeStraw

A LifeStraw personal water filtration system is another little gizmo that will make you feel like you are an extreme survivalist and world adventurer. When you pull water through a LifeStraw, it filters the water so it is drinkable. A LifeStraw will protect you from bacteria, parasites, and microplastics.

I not only have one of these in my bug-out bag but also travel with one internationally and even within the US. It weighs less than two ounces, and chances are I will never need it. But if I do need it, I will be so grateful to have carried those two ounces with me.

D. Boiling Water

If you feel that your water may be compromised and you have the capability, boiling water will help kill any nasty parasites that may be present. The water must be boiled rapidly at a full boil for three minutes to protect against disease.

E. Another Way to Conserve Water

During a water crisis, you will also want to "double up" your water usage. For example, when using water to boil pasta, reserve the water you drain from the pasta and use it for watering plants, quick-boiling broccoli, or any other use that doesn't require 100 percent pristine (but still consumable) water.

WHERE TO PUT ALL THAT WATER

When it comes to water storage, after the container, the next most important thing is location, location, location.

Think about any unused space in your home, then think about whether the water will be safe there. A good storage place for jugs or tanks should be dark, cool, and out of the way but not so hard to get to that it would be difficult to access in an emergency.

Places where you could store water include these:

- garage
- basement
- under a stairwell
- in the closet of a spare room
- under the beds

If you live in a tiny space, you will have to get super creative. You may have to consider some unconventional spots:

- on the bottom shelf of a bookcase
- under the bathroom sink
- behind furniture (especially the water jugs)

Now is an excellent time to get rid of things you don't need in order to store the stuff you do need for an emergency.

YOUR PLAN

Write down your plan for water storage. Include containers and other equipment you need to buy and what you need to do to clear space in your home to store them.

Again, make sure you set a deadline for completion of this project.

FOURTEEN

PREP #11:
PREP YOUR TEAM

One of the most valuable things you will do to be ready for anything is build a team of people who will help each other get ready.

Roger's favorite place—except for in my loving embrace (and I'm guessing even that probably comes in at number two)—is Disneyland. The last time we visited Disneyland, we were on our way to use our Fast Pass at Radiator Springs when my stomach started to feel upset. Really upset. After a few minutes, I asked Roger to head to the hotel to get me some Tums while I sat on a bench way too close to a churro stand for someone who was feeling sick to her stomach.

While Roger was away, I spiraled. My stomach churned, sweat drenched my shirt, and waves of nausea and dizziness took over. Once my husband was back and saw that I was getting worse, he flagged down a cast member to get help. I finally did the unthinkable and lay down on a park bench in the middle of California Adventure. I was too sick to be completely mortified.

Within thirty seconds, I could hear a cast member asking Roger questions. (I couldn't talk at all.) Besides getting my age wrong (thanks for the extra year, Roger), he was able to give them all the information they required. About a minute later, two nurses showed up with a wheelchair and took my vitals. One nurse asked the other to redo my blood pressure. It was low. Dangerously low. Then, while the first nurse did a blood draw, I heard someone say, "The paramedics are here!"

Eventually I was able to sit up and open my eyes. And the scene around me was both overwhelming and impressive: Two nurses taking my vitals. Four paramedics ready to whisk me off to the hospital. Five cast members standing like centurions, moving people along and keeping them from sitting on the very long bench where I was having my moment.

I said I didn't feel like I needed the ambulance, thank you very much. But I accepted the wheelchair ride back to the nurse's station. (During my worst time, all I kept thinking was, *I'm in the middle of the park, how do I get out of here?* That wheelchair was the most beautiful thing I'd seen all day.)

The ride back to the nurse's station was also an experience. One cast member walked ahead of us and kept demanding in a firm but controlled voice, "Keep to the right! Wheelchair coming through." A security guard pushed my wheelchair, and the nurse, whom I now knew as Candace, walked right beside me. Another cast member walked with Roger behind me and asked questions.

At the nurse's center, they had a bed and a room waiting. Candace took my blood pressure again, and it was getting back up to human levels.

After about an hour in the nurse's room, where I drank a

full bottle of water, Candace took us out to the drop-off area, where we grabbed an Uber and went back to the hotel. I then slept for twelve hours straight.

Turns out, I was simply dehydrated. I've now learned to carry a bottle of water with me wherever I go (and actually drink it).

The other thing I learned? When it comes to an emergency, I want to be as prepared as Uncle Walt and everyone who works for the mouse. The cast members were so impressive. No one had to ask anyone else questions, decide what their roles were, or discuss what was going to happen next. Everyone knew their roles and performed them without question.

This experience at Disneyland convinced me to step up my game plan. Roger and I now have regular discussions about who will do what in case of an emergency.

We should all have these discussions to determine who is going to do what when an emergency happens. Decide who is in charge of the following tasks:

- getting the kids out of the house
- securing important papers and documents (if they are not stored off-site)
- getting the pets out of the house
- providing first aid
- planning meals
- taking care of finances

When you know who is in charge of what area during an emergency, it is one more thing you can check off your list. You know that someone you trust has it under control.

■   ■   ■

It was the perfect night.

The last day of March with evening temperatures in the midsixties. The steaks were on the smoker, and I made an amazing bacon and broccoli salad. Until the steaks were done, we sat around the fire with some of our best friends, Scott and Kelli, and talked about church and kids and home renovations and work while munching on Marco Polo cheese from Beecher's in Seattle.

Perfect.

Then, over fruit tarts and chocolate ganache cake (I told you it was perfect), we made plans for where we would try to meet up if a major earthquake hit Northern California.

Welcome to zombie apocalypse training with the Lipps.

Kelli and Scott, besides being our friends and Scott being our pastor, are the people we've teamed up with to do life, come what may. If they have an emergency at their home, they don't need to hustle to find somewhere to stay—they already have a code to our house and know where the towels are. If a pipe bursts in our house and we have to get out with just the clothes on our backs and our pets? We'd head to Scott and Kelli's.

The four of us meet once a month. During these dinners, we talk about where we are in our emergency planning, how we can get better prepared, how we are doing on our 3-2-3 goals, and what we would do in an actual emergency. These dinners are not doom-and-gloom discussions about protecting our homes and making barricades. Instead, we talk about how we can be ready if one of us loses our job, how we can be of service to each other, and how we can be of service to others in the event of a disaster.

Why is having others on your team so important?

1. We are better together. In the case of a disaster, we have two other people who will drop anything to help. We have been there for each other in the past through small things, like giving rides to pick up cars from the mechanic, to big things, like helping prepare our mountain house for renters. We can rely on them, and they can rely on us.

   Plus, Kelli and Scott have different talents than Roger and I do. In an emergency, Scott can repair a lot of things that Roger and I wouldn't have a clue how to fix. Scott has taught CPR and first aid, so he's valuable during an emergency. Roger can create communication systems in a disaster. Kelli knows a ton about homes and has a great analytical mind. She thinks things through and asks the right questions. And me? Well, I can make a three-course dinner out of a package of ramen noodles and a can of green beans.

   These are the people I want on my team.

2. We understand each other's goals. This planning isn't just for when a fire hits—it's for when Roger or Scott loses a job, or Kelli or I (both being self-employed) have a year when we don't make much money.

3. We are motivated to think beyond ourselves.

   When something is going on in Scott and Kelli's life, I want to be one of the first to know about it so I can be one of the first to serve. Plus, when someone we know is going through a difficult circumstance, the four of us can team up and serve better.

YOUR PLAN

Who can you team up with to be ready for anything? Schedule a meeting with prospective partners to discuss how you can help each other prepare and what your roles might be. Keep in mind the willingness of those who are living with you in your household and their particular strengths. You'll get much more enthusiastic help if you approach them in the right way (see the introduction).

Write the date of your meeting in your Ready for Anything notebook, and during the meeting, jot down notes of decisions made and the date of your next meeting.

FIFTEEN

PREP #12: GET YOUR SUPPLIES TOGETHER

Question 1: Do you have an emergency kit? Question 2: Do you actually know where it is? Question 3: Are the adhesive bandages older than your youngest kid? If you've answered no to either of the first two questions or yes to the third, then this chapter is for you.

Recently I cut my finger while chopping onions. This was after, earlier in the day, I cut my finger chopping eggs.

Now when Roger sees me with a cutting board, he immediately leaves the room. But that day I was so glad we both knew exactly where the first aid kit was. I will confess that it had Scooby-Doo bandages in it, and our youngest child is twenty-six. Neither of us remember buying those particular bandages, but it turns out Scooby holds up pretty well. (We had newer bandages in there, but tightwad that I am, I had to see if they would still work.)

All of us need to be prepared not only for when the next ouchie happens but for the next time we have a problem beyond day-to-day scratches and boo-boos.

PUTTING TOGETHER YOUR KIT

There is no shame in going to the store and buying a ready-made emergency kit. In fact, that is exactly what I have done. But if you already have a lot of the following supplies on hand and just need to freshen up your kit, here is a checklist from the Red Cross[1] of items you should have:

- 2 absorbent compress dressings (5" × 9")
- 25 adhesive bandages (assorted sizes)
- 1 adhesive cloth tape (10 yds. × 1")
- 5 antibiotic ointment packets
- 5 antiseptic wipe packets
- 2 packets of aspirin (81 mg each)
- 1 emergency blanket
- 1 breathing barrier (with one-way valve)
- 1 instant cold compress
- 2 pairs of nonlatex gloves (size large)
- 2 hydrocortisone ointment packets
- 1 3" gauze roll (roller) bandage
- 1 4" gauze roll (roller) bandage
- 5 sterile gauze pads (3" × 3")
- 5 sterile gauze pads (4" × 4")
- Oral thermometer (nonmercury/nonglass)
- 2 triangular bandages
- tweezers
- emergency first aid guide

---

1. "Make a First Aid Kit," The Red Cross, https://www.redcross.org/get-help /how-to-prepare-for-emergencies/anatomy-of-a-first-aid-kit.html.

Make sure that everything you have in your kit is in working order and is not outdated. In an emergency, you will be grateful for a cold compress that actually gets cold when you need it.

Roger and I each have a kit in our cars, and we have one downstairs, on the top shelf of our hall closet, which is right next to the kitchen. In the mountains, we have a larger kit plus a backpacking kit just in case someone is hurt on our property and we need to hike to get to them.

OTHER MEDICINES AND PRESCRIPTIONS

I take prescription medicine on a daily basis. It is important for my health that I not go more than a day or two without it, so I have made a plan to have it with me in an emergency. I have a three-day supply in my bug-out bag and keep the pills in a prescription bottle so I have all the information I need to get the prescription refilled as quickly as possible.

Some prescriptions can't be refilled until the user is almost out of medication, but I refill mine as early as possible. Always be sure to have your prescription called in, and be ready to pick it up as soon as it's available. Ask your doctor if it's possible to request renewals sooner. (I did this once for a prescription I was taking on an extended trip.) You could also ask the doctor for samples to complete your emergency supply.

Another prescription you may want to consider is your eyeglasses. I have an old pair of prescription glasses and sunglasses packed in my bug-out bag. If we leave in the middle of the night and I'm not wearing my regular pair of glasses, I want to make sure I can do things that require wearing my glasses, like driving, and, well . . . seeing.

I recommend having a backup pair of glasses anyway. As someone who has had glasses break, trust me, you don't want to pay the price to expedite an order of new prescription glasses. You won't be able to see through all the tears when you see the cost. And wearing your sunglasses 24/7 until your new glasses are ready? That only works for Bono.

OVER-THE-COUNTER MEDS

If you are ever in Northern California and feeling less than awesome, come to my house. I promise you, at all times, I have over-the-counter medications for all these common ailments:

- common cold
- aches and pain
- fever
- diarrhea
- nausea
- upset stomach
- allergies
- cough
- sinus congestion
- constipation

The last thing you want to do when you're feeling icky? Run to the store to pick up the medication you need.

And while having these on hand for an emergency is a great idea (and having one or two of each in your car emergency kit is a total win), I like to have them around for day-to-day use as well. Because guaranteed, within a twelve-month time span, we will experience eight of these issues (especially since I'm married to Allergy Boy).

Please consult with your doctor about what kinds of over-the-counter medications are best for you. But be well prepared for whatever medical issue (big or small) comes your way.

PERSONAL HYGIENE

One of our favorite family stories dates back to when my mom and dad were newlyweds. My mom was getting ready for work and was in the middle of brushing her teeth with an electric toothbrush. Back in the day, apparently, there was no charger. You would actually have to plug the cord for the toothbrush into the wall.

Well, my parents' power went out, and there was my mom, standing there with the electric toothbrush, crying out to my dad, "Oh no! How am I going to finish brushing my teeth for work?"

It never occurred to my mom that she could manually brush her teeth with an electric toothbrush.

During an emergency situation, you may not have all the comforts that would normally surround you at home, but you will quickly figure out ways to adapt and keep yourself reasonably clean and healthy.

When it comes to your two-week supply of personal hygiene items, my suggestion is to have a two-week stock of whatever you normally use on hand at home. These items will include the following:

- toothpaste and toothbrush
- floss

- shampoo and conditioner
- deodorant
- facial cleanser
- soap
- body wash
- cotton swabs
- toilet paper
- razor
- feminine hygiene supplies

And then I would suggest you have more than what you would normally use of a few other items:

- dry shampoo (in case you are without water)
- personal cleansing wipes (again, in case you are without water; and they will also save on laundering washcloths, towels, etc.)

LAUNDRY SUPPLIES

The thing that got me started on this whole prepping journey was an internet search about how to do laundry when you don't have a washer while on vacation. I have now done my laundry without a washer several times and have learned a few tricks along the way.

Before we get to the hows of doing laundry during an emergency, I want you to think through your everyday, non-emergency approach to doing laundry.

I used to be a saver-upper when it came to laundry. I would wait until I had full loads of every type (and in my brain, there were about eight different loads, including dress shirts, whites, colors, underwear and socks, towels and jeans, sweats, kitchen linens, bedding, and delicates.)

This worked fine for a while. But then came the day when a speaker friend got sick and I had to fill in for her at the last minute. I had to pack for a trip that would include three days of speaking. All my "good" clothes were in the dirty clothes hamper. My best options were a Disneyland '06 T-shirt and a pair of yoga pants with only one hole in them.

Yes, I did get some clothes quickly washed and packed. And I learned from the experience. Now, instead of waiting around until my hamper is bursting at the seams, I like to stay on top of my loads so that when the next crisis comes around (jeans that don't fit like they did two weeks ago), I have options. And I have eliminated another emergency in my life.

In an emergency situation, however, you will want to approach laundry differently than you would in your noncrisis life. When the power is out or water is a luxury, your attitude, and your family's attitude, about laundry must radically change.

When my kids were teenagers, laundry was a hot-button issue. With six of us in the house, full loads piled up quickly, and I would do everyone's laundry at the same time. That is, until one day I went to the hamper, and there was my son's shirt, still folded, sitting on top of the dirty laundry. For him, it was easier to put the shirt in the hamper than to put it away. And that's the day I stopped doing everyone else's laundry.

As I said, in a crisis situation, everyone needs to take a radically different view of laundry:

1. **Wear clothes more than once.** I love putting on a fresh shirt and pants every day, but in a crisis situation, I'm going to have to be okay with wearing my clothes more than once.

2. **Wash underwear and socks daily.** I can get through anything in life as long as I have clean underwear. During a crisis, you will want to stay on top of washing things like underwear, socks, and undershirts on a regular basis. Those make for smallish loads and are much easier to stay on top of than bulkier items like sweatshirts and jeans.

3. **Stay on top of stains.** Instead of throwing jeans in the wash because they have a stain on them, use a Tide To Go instant stain remover pen or a Shout Wipe & Go to stay on top of stains.

OTHER SUPPLIES

People who travel in RVs or live on boats or in cabins have been doing off-grid clothes washing for years. The advances in compact, no-electricity, low-water washing machines are amazing. If you are living in a situation where off-grid laundry is more likely than not, you may want to consider something like the Wonder Wash nonelectric, portable compact washing machine. This helpful tool will do small loads of laundry much more easily than doing them by hand.

But if you are saving your survival pennies for canned meats right now and not new laundry systems, you can get laundry done with a few items from around the house.

Here are some things to have on hand to make off-grid laundry easier:

1. **Scrub brush.** For tough stains, you still want to use a stain treatment, but you can combine that with a scrub brush to get out tough stains (since you won't be using an agitator on a washing machine to do the work for you).

2. **Bucket with lid.** Having a five-gallon bucket to wash a small load of clothes in is going to be a huge help. If you want to get really fancy, have two buckets. I have a five-gallon bucket with a lid, and for emergencies, I have the mop bucket I use on my floors that I can clean out, giving me two buckets, one for washing and one for rinsing. In the bucket you will use for washing clothes, cut a hole in the lid for the agitator.

3. **Agitator.** You are going to need something to agitate the clothes with in order to get them clean. You can use a new, untainted plunger to do the job or a hand-powered clothes washing wand. Or get an old-fashioned wash board.

4. **Washing detergent.** You can buy store detergent or make your own. (Instructions to follow at the end of the chapter.)

5. **Drying system.** By "system" I mean a way to dry clothes that works for you. Nine months out of the year, I dry most of my clothes by air to save on electricity— and because sun-dried clothes are awesome.

Having a clothesline and some clothespins on hand will make drying easier in most months of the year.

For sunless days, I set up a rack in our bathtub to dry small clothes on and then hang shirts on hangers from the shower curtain rod. Almost always those clothes dry overnight as long as I don't scrunch them together. And yes, the T-shirts do come out a little stiff. But there is no need for dryer sheets when you are air-drying—the clothes soften up within five minutes of wearing them.

The four steps you need to master for washing your clothes are as follows:

1. Prepping

   In nonemergency times, you might be a laundry all-star if you actually pretreat a stain. But in an off-grid situation, you will need to be a little more careful:

   ○ Shake. Yes, shake your clothes. This will get any extra dirt off so you can use as little water as possible.

   ○ Treat stains. Treat stains as quickly as possible to keep them from setting in. Use the scrub brush we talked about and pay special attention to the underarm areas of shirts.

   ○ Soak. Soaking your clothes (just as you would with a presoak setting on a washing machine) will loosen up soil and get your garments that much cleaner. Just fill a bucket with (preferably warm) water and laundry soap.

   ○ Use the right detergent. I've included my recipe for homemade high-efficiency (HE) laundry detergent, which is perfect for off-grid laundry since it is low-sudsing, which is what you want so you don't have to waste water on rinsing. Plus, soaking cleans your clothes without extra work from you. Win-win!

   Once the soap is dissolved, add in the clothes and let them soak for thirty minutes to work on any stubborn stains.

2. Washing

After soaking, start agitating the clothes, soap, and water in the same bucket. Be sure to put the lid back on the bucket with the hole cut out for the agitator. You are going to be working hard to get those clothes clean, and the last thing you want to do is mop up your house after washing clothes. Ring out as much of the soapy water as possible.

3. Rinsing

Getting as much of the soap out of your clothes as possible by rinsing them is important (especially if your family deals with skin irritations or allergies). Pull the clothes out of the first bucket, letting as much dirty water and soap drip off as possible. Then, using your second bucket, use half of your clean water to rinse the clothes and the other half to rinse again.

4. Wringing

You don't have to wring your clothes, but it will make the drying process go much faster. I use rubber gardening gloves to wring out the clothes. You will be surprised how much work it takes.

Here are the supplies you need for off-grid laundry:

- laundry soap
- Woolite
- clothesline
- clothespins

- two buckets
- Tide To Go pen
- Small sewing kit

DIY HIGH-EFFICIENCY LAUNDRY SOAP

I'd heard of people making their own liquid laundry detergent, but because there was mixing and boiling involved, I thought, *Ugh, no thank you.* But when I read how much money people were saving by making their own detergent, each time I picked up a giant tub of suds at a warehouse store and had to pay way too much money, it made my budget very, very sad.

So when I came across this powdered laundry detergent recipe, I knew I had to give it a try. It smells great, works great, is super easy to make, and I can get all the ingredients for under thirty-five dollars. And it lasts for at least six months.

The first question everyone asks me is "Are you sure it's safe for high-efficiency washers?" I have scoured the internet looking for anyone who has had a problem with it, and have yet to find anyone. The main concern is that HE washers require a less-sudsy detergent. Well, I've watched my laundry go through a cycle with both the store-bought HE detergent and this homemade version (no, I don't have better things to do with my time), and the sudsing was identical. But if you are of the super-paranoid variety, twelve dollars a month is a small price to pay for peace of mind. My hubby is very skeptical of "alternative" anything, but even he was convinced to give homemade detergent a try. So far we are loving it. By the way, we've been using this recipe for more than six years and have never had a problem.

HOMEMADE HIGH-EFFICIENCY LAUNDRY DETERGENT

Ingredients

3 bars Fels-Naptha, grated ($1.33 × 3)

1 box Borax ($5.75 for 76 ounces)

1 box Washing Soda ($4.00 for 55 ounces)

2 cups baking soda ($0.65)

2 containers powdered OxiClean ($12.99 for 7.2 pounds)

1–2 containers of Purex fabric softener crystals ($6.97 for 28 ounces). One bottle is plenty of scent for my gang.

We found all of the ingredients to make homemade HE laundry detergent at Target and on Amazon. I was impatient to try this out, so I bought all the ingredients right away. Now I watch for them to go on sale to try to keep the price down even more.

Directions

1. Start by grating the Fels-Naptha. I see that most people do this with a hand grater, but the soap is not that hard, and I was able to use my food processor to grate it. Most people want it more grated (and would use a different blade), but I loved the cheesy look of it.

2. Next, mix grated soap and the rest of your ingredients together. It seems that most people mixed right into the tub where they were going to store their soap. I wanted to make sure it got completely mixed up, so I used a big

> black trash bag to line my bucket and poured every-
> thing in there. (Another hint: do this outside for better
> ventilation; the powder scent is strong.)
>
> 3. Gather the top of the trash bag and keep tossing the
>   ingredients over and over until fully mixed.
> 4. Store soap in a sealed container with a scoop. I transfer
>   what I'll need for a month into a smaller jar to keep in
>   my laundry area. Use 2 tablespoons of detergent for
>   every load of laundry. Make sure to put the detergent
>   directly into the tub and not in the detergent dispenser.

I love so many things about this homemade detergent. It is the ultimate clutter-free way to do laundry.

IT'S CHEAPER: By making this at home, I save over $100 a year.

LESS PACKAGING: It's better for the environment.

LESS LUGGING: I hate with a fiery passion dragging all those giant items home from a warehouse store but love that I can pick up these small items and keep the tub in my garage.

NEVER RUNNING OUT OF LAUNDRY SOAP: Priceless.

This chapter is all about being safe and clean. We all understand the need for safety in an emergency, but never underestimate the power of feeling clean in a crisis. I promise, it will be worth all the effort to have clean underwear and will give you the strength to go on.

YOUR PLAN

Write in your Ready for Anything notebook your plan for supplying an emergency first aid kit, hygiene supplies, and laundry supplies. As you plan, record any items you need to buy on your grocery lists.

Make sure you include a deadline for purchasing and preparing these items.

CHAPTER SIXTEEN

PREP #13:
PREP YOUR KIDS

As a parent, your whole view on prepping changes. It's no longer just you, and potentially a spouse, you are prepping for. Add a kid to the mix, and prepping takes on a whole new list of items and tasks.

The most important thing I would say about prepping your kids is that you have the chance to raise humans who don't fear what is going to happen. You can teach them that with a combination of trusting God and taking responsibility for themselves, their family, and those around them, they can face the future without fear. And one of the big steps to helping your kids live a life with less fear is to talk through your plans for when something happens.

Your kids don't need to be burdened with all the possible scenarios of what could happen in an emergency. What they need to know is what you want them to do when an emergency happens.

For kids, prepping is a lot like the fire drills we all participated in during school. In kindergarten the drills were maybe a little scary but mostly exciting. By the time we reached high school, we just stood around and talked to our friends because we knew what to do in an emergency. We want our kids to have the confidence to move forward without fear.

When an emergency hits, your kids should also be ready for anything.

PRACTICE

One of the best ways to prepare your kids is by practicing. Give your child (and yourself) opportunities to live without power, water, and other things we all take for granted.

Recently I talked with a friend, Sarah, who told me about someone she knows who is training to be a missionary. She's doing her training in San Diego. My first thought was, *San Diego? I would want to train there too!* But then I found out that the training organization prepares them to live on the mission field by randomly turning off their power or water so they will know how to do without when they actually arrive at their assignment.

This is what we can do with our families as well. What would we do for an evening without any electricity? How would we cook, work, do chores, and entertain ourselves? Give yourself and your kids the opportunity to figure this out before a disaster happens. Who knows, you may all find that you enjoy cooking on the grill and playing board games by candlelight as much as you enjoy Netflix. (Okay, that's a long shot.)

Another way to practice with your family is to go camping. Camping is the ultimate prepper prep. You have to think through everything you'll need for a night, a week, or longer.

If you're packing for a night of camping, you might as well stay for three nights. Packing for one night of camping is like paying for a professional hairstyle, donning a new formal gown with matching shoes, and then going for drive-through tacos. You don't want to put in all that effort for such a quick trip. You might as well stay out for a good while to get the most out of your preparations.

By camping, you and your kids will learn how to do all your daily living chores off grid. So when a crisis occurs when you're at home, as the parent, all you have to say to your child is, "Remember what we did when we were camping? That's how we're going to make breakfast today." In a crisis, give your kids a point of reference to hold on to so they have the security of knowing they've done this before and they will be okay.

SKILLS

I grew up without a lot of the day-to-day skills that would be helpful in a crisis situation. If you needed to know the names of everyone on the *Brady Bunch* or *Eight Is Enough*, I was your girl. But practical life skills? Not so much.

Give your kids a running start so they possess the skills that will help them become mature adults. One of the greatest gifts we can give our kids is to instill in them the knowledge that they are capable human beings who can take care of themselves. Scouting programs are great places to learn self-sufficiency, teamwork, and preparedness. Everyday tasks at home can also give your kids the skills they need to navigate an emergency.

Here are some skills that kids (when age appropriate)

should have. And if you don't have them, this is a great time to learn alongside your kids. By the way, none of these skills should be separated out as "skills for boys" and "skills for girls." Even though my husband and I have certain skill sets and comfort levels with different tasks, I need to know how to do everything in case of an emergency:

- basic first aid
- building a fire
- cooking on a grill or camp stove
- basic sewing skills
- cleaning (bathrooms, kitchen, food prep areas)

As much as these skills will serve your child in a crisis, these are skills that they will need to function in the real world.

When my daughter came home from college the first time, she shared how shocked she was by how little the other college students could do for themselves. "Mom," she exclaimed, "I'm having to teach bunches of people how to do laundry! How do you get through eighteen years of life and not know how to do laundry?"

Don't let your child be the kid at college whom other students have to teach to do laundry. Send capable adults into the world by raising competent kids.

INFORMATION

Your kids should know where you keep your emergency supplies, as well as your emergency binder containing your household information, and so should anyone who is taking care of your kids in your home, including babysitters and grandparents.

Make your kids the gophers when it comes to tasks like grabbing food from your two-week rotation or finding a flashlight when you're going on a walk. Your kids need to know where all your stuff is so that if they are home without you, they can fend for themselves until you are reunited.

One of the most important ways to prepare your child for an emergency is to consider who they are spending their time with when they are not with you. In a disaster, you may not be able to get to your child right away if you are at work or they are at school. Do you have confidence that the people you are leaving your child with will have your child's best interests in mind in an emergency? Have you been informed of their emergency procedures?

My daughter Amanda is the director of a preschool whose staff takes emergency procedures seriously. If a parent asks her what happens in the case of an earthquake, she doesn't have to go look up the school's procedure in a binder. She and her team are ready for any emergency and can assure parents that their kids will be taken care of no matter what the circumstances.

Make sure that you feel confident in those whom your kids are spending time with. It may be hours (or, God forbid, days) before you can get to your kids safely. Know that they are already in the best hands (besides yours) possible.

Pass on any important information to those entrusted with your kids' care, such as alternative methods of reaching you, other people authorized to pick them up, and medical needs.

For example, if you normally administer medication outside school hours but an emergency prevents teachers and students from leaving for a long period of time, your child's teacher will need to have a backup supply of that medication and know when and how to administer it.

Communication is key when preparing your kids for an emergency in the event that they are not with you.

SHOWING YOUR OWN RESILIENCY

My aunt Vina lived in her own upstairs apartment into her nineties. Not all of us will be blessed with such physical and mental longevity, but I believe that growing our resiliency is one of the things we can do to surprise ourselves with our own capabilities and to get our kids to expand their belief in their capabilities.

As I mentioned earlier, one of the reasons I started down this path of preparedness is because I didn't feel capable of taking care of myself. Yes, I was able to feed myself, bathe myself, and generally function as an adult when all circumstances went according to plan. But when the power or water went out, I was at a total loss. I wanted to show not only myself that I was a capable human being but to show my kids that they could be capable as well.

We have created a society in which we depend on others to take care of all our problems. One of the best gifts you can give your kids is to let them know that they can take care of themselves when there is a problem by taking care of yourself.

Even though my kids are grown, it is important for them to see their parent being capable.

YOUR PLAN

Plan a fun outing with your kids that includes learning at least one survival skill. As long as you keep it fun, your children will learn to deal confidently with contingencies and you will create great family memories. It's a win-win.

Set a date for a meeting with your spouse (or other person who supports your parenting) to assess which skills your kids need to learn, and write the list in your notebook. Beside each item, write the date you want to have this training accomplished. Plan for camping trips, hiking, and other outdoor activities. Include your children in daily household tasks such as laundry, cleaning, and yard work.

SEVENTEEN

PREP #14:
PREP YOUR TECH

It was one of those fun opportunities that doesn't come up very often for me and my hubby.

Roger was attending a technical conference at the Moscone Center in downtown San Francisco. Because Roger was having knee surgery the following week and walking caused him pain, we had to stay in a hotel close to the conference center. The closest hotel happened to be very swanky. (Normally we find the nearest Holiday Inn Express and call it a day.)

Naturally, I didn't want that hotel room to go to waste, so I tagged along and used the time as a mini writing retreat while Roger was at the conference. And bonus? My brother Brian worked nearby, so I was able to meet him, my sister-in-law Lucinda, and our niece for lunch.

After a morning of writing, I met my family for burgers. Brian had to go back to work, so Lucinda, Elsa, and I spent the next couple of hours exploring the city by foot. When it was time for the two of them to head back for the train home,

Lucinda asked if they could stop at our hotel room so they could use the bathroom first.

When we got to the room, we ran into the housekeeper who was about to tidy it up. I asked if she could wait five minutes while we all used the facilities. As we left the room, I held the door open for the housekeeper. Then I walked Lucinda and our niece to the train station. Afterward, I planned to do a little shopping.

When I came back to the hotel to work and then get ready to meet Roger for dinner, my computer wasn't in my room where I'd left it.

I was sure that my husband, who is much more naturally conscientious than I am, must have come back during a break in the conference and taken the computer off the little desk in the room and put it somewhere "safe."

But now I couldn't find that "safe" place, so I texted Roger.

"Have you been back to our hotel room?"

"Ha! Yes—did I leave footprints behind?"

"Ha! I'm so relieved. Can you tell me where you put my laptop?"

"I didn't move it. The last I saw it, it was on the desk."

"Um . . . Okay . . . I think someone stole my laptop . . ."

"I'm coming back now."

Sure enough, my computer had been stolen out of our room in the super swanky hotel.

After a lot of back-and-forth with the hotel manager, who accused my sister-in-law of taking the computer, we realized what had happened.

While the hotel maid was cleaning the room, a woman popped in and said, "Oh, you're still cleaning? I'll just work downstairs." She then grabbed my computer and walked straight out of the hotel.

So what started as a fun writing adventure in a posh hotel room ended with police officers in that same posh hotel room after midnight. (The SFPD didn't exactly rush right over like you see in the movies. Since their patrol area was right next to the Tenderloin District of San Francisco, my laptop being stolen likely wasn't the biggest crime of their night.)

Now, having your stuff stolen is never fun. You have a feeling of weirdness and violation as you walk through the world and realize just how vulnerable you are. And to know that someone could walk in off the streets into your room and grab your stuff? Well, that's just creepy.

But the good news? My computer was ready for anything.

Technology and security change so rapidly, it would be impossible for me to get specific and technical in a book that has a shelf life longer than three months. But my laptop had some general safety precautions that every tech owner should be employing.

- **It was password protected.** Every time I want to work on my computer, I have to log into it with a password. The average thief off the street (from what we were told by the police officers and my daughter who works for Apple) couldn't get any personal data from the laptop. Instead, they were probably planning on selling it for parts. They wouldn't likely bother trying to access information because the computer was password protected.
- **We have a password management program.** We use a program called Dashlane that offers a safe, simple

way to store passwords and personal information. My husband and I share an account, and we have people on our business team who have different access levels to our information. This way we are not emailing passwords back and forth to each other or keeping sensitive data on our computers. Everything is secure through Dashlane.

- **Everything was backed up on Dropbox.** We use Dropbox to back up all our files automatically. I don't even have to think about it. (Which is a good thing, because back in the day when we had to remember to back things up, I rarely remembered to do so.)

So even though my laptop was stolen and it was a hassle to get the hotel's insurance to pay for it (which they eventually did), the amazing news?

I lost exactly two documents.

Two.

I had typed out some brainstorming notes on a couple of ideas and hadn't saved them (because they were just quick ideas). Those were the only things I lost even though my computer was stolen.

We had no security breaches. No one broke into our bank account. None of our personal identity was exposed. None of my work (I was in the middle of editing a book) was lost. As someone who is walking through the world post–laptop thievery, I feel so much safer and securer knowing that the tools we have in place really work.

You can do a number of things to make sure your tech is ready for anything.

LAPTOP

Remember the three heroes in my hotel story?

- password protection
- password management (Dashlane)
- automated backup (Dropbox)

These three items made it so that I was only without my hardware, never without my data.

PHONE

Have Emergency Info on Your Phone

I have an app on my phone called Emergency ID (free). It's an Android app, but for you iPhone users, you have the Health app that does almost exactly the same thing.

What I love about this app is that it floats an icon over my lock screen, so even though the rest of the contents of my phone are behind a lock screen, my emergency medical information (what meds I'm taking, my blood type, any allergies or other necessary info), is right at a friend's or emergency responder's fingertips. It also lets emergency responders know that I'm an organ donor so they can take appropriate action to get my body to the right place in case I'm no longer using it.

This app also has a section with first aid techniques. While nothing replaces taking a first aid course, having this guide as a refresher is a great resource.

Find My Phone Feature

If any of your devices are ever lost or stolen, you can locate them with this app. If necessary, you can remotely lock the device or erase the data to prevent security breaches. All you need to do is enable "Find my iPhone" for an Apple device or "Find my device" for Android.

Have a Backup Charger

I have a pretty long battery life on my phone, but sometimes (especially when I'm using my phone as a hot spot for my laptop), I run out of battery and I'm not able to plug in. A variety of phone chargers (including solar chargers) are sold anywhere you purchase phone accessories.

ABC—Always Be Charging

And my number one piece of advice when it comes to your tech stuff? ABC—always be charging.

Don't you love it when you're watching a movie and the main character gets a call from an unknown number in the middle of the night, rolls over, grabs their phone, and groggily answers, "Hello?"

A few things . . .

1. Why do you have your ringer on unless your teenager is out later than you stay up? Otherwise, keep that puppy on silent.
2. Why are you answering an unknown number? I have those numbers blocked because nobody in the history of blocked numbers has ever called to say, "I love you!" or offer money.

3. Why are those phones never charging? They are just lying there on the nightstand, magically 100 percent charged all the time.

But in the real, nonmovie world, the rest of us need to be charging. And charging, whenever you can, is a way to be ready for anything. In a crisis situation, the last thing you want to happen is to run out of battery life when you are trying to connect with everyone you love. So throughout your day, think about all the places you could be charging your phone, computer, smart watch, tablet, and other electronics.

1. Have a charging station on your nightstand for your phone, backup battery, and watch.
2. Have a charging station for your tablet and laptop wherever you use them most.
3. Have a charging station at work, preferably not one that you have to drag back and forth from home. Even leaving it in a locked drawer or locker is a better plan than having to transport it every day.
4. Charge your phone in your car while driving.
5. Carry a backup battery in your computer bag or purse to always have an extra supply of juice on hand.

You may think I'm a bit obsessive about charging my gear, but since words are my business, I know how disappointing it is to have a chunk of time to work but no computer to write with, no phone to connect with. You're probably just as reliant on your devices for your job.

GET YOUR TECH READY FOR ANYTHING

Having your devices lost or stolen is a bummer. And it's down-right maddening when they crash. But if you take the steps outlined in this chapter, you can decrease your frustration. Whether your devices end up in a posh hotel or out in the woods in a backpack, you'll be ready for anything.

YOUR PLAN

Make a list of all the devices you own and write them down in your Ready for Anything notebook. If multiple people need access to the passwords, create a Dashlane account.

For each device, create a checklist:

- password protected
- Dropbox downloaded
- emergency information uploaded
- "Find my device" enabled
- backup chargers purchased
- date for completing checklist noted

EIGHTEEN

PREP #15: GATHER YOUR TOOLS

I would say that 95 percent of this book is just common sense laid out in an easy-to-follow format. And the last 5 percent? Things I found on the internet that would be valuable in certain emergency situations. Some are items I wouldn't discuss at dinner parties because people would think I've become a survivalist—or lost my mind. Or those who overheard would be the first to show up at my house when a disaster strikes.

Nevertheless, I do think the following tools merit your consideration.

NOAA WEATHER RADIO

This weather alert radio will keep you up to date on weather-related situations in your area, such as hurricanes, tornadoes, and severe storms. It is a lifesaver when your power is out and you need to know about current weather conditions and alerts from local authorities. I suggest one with a lamp or flashlight, solar or another charging system (including hand cranking).

My number one reason for having a NOAA weather radio is to know when I should shelter in place and when I should plan on leaving my home in a disaster.

WATERBOB

As mentioned in chapter 13, a WaterBOB is an emergency water storage container for your bathtub. If you know a disaster is coming, put the WaterBOB in your bathtub and fill it up. Seal it, and you will have up to one hundred gallons of clean drinking water ready to go.

LIFESTRAW

If you read the book or watched the movie *Wild: From Lost to Found on the Pacific Crest Trail* by Cheryl Strayed, you know the importance of having clean, drinkable water. I knew about the LifeStraw while I was reading that book and wanted to magically teleport the handy little device to our heroine. The LifeStraw, as described earlier, is basically a personal filter so that you can have clean drinking water anywhere. It can filter up to a thousand gallons of contaminated water and turn it into clean and safe drinking water.

TARPS

While living for six months in the mountains (which is basically like glamping) while renovating our home in the city, I discovered the wonder of tarps. These plastic lifesavers covered our cut wood, became a sled to pull it through the snow, and served as a clean place to lie down while digging our car tires out of the mud. Having a tarp in the car and another at the house is something you will never regret.

FOLDABLE SHOVEL

We've only had a foldable shovel for less than a year, but we have already used it to dig out of snow. I'm so glad we had it, or we might still be stuck! A foldable shovel is small enough to fit easily into your trunk. You won't regret purchasing this small but mighty tool.

ROPE

Having a length of heavy-duty rope in your car and at your house is a great idea for many types of emergencies.

SOLAR CHARGER

If power outages are common in your area, you would be crazy not to have a small solar charger. We have a small panel that can run an electric cooler or fan, and a couple of tiny panels that can recharge our cell phones.

SELF-CONTAINED STOVE

Having a place to heat up the food you've stored is vital not only so you can eat during a disaster but also because it offers a sense of comfort and normalcy during a difficult time. Most canned foods can be eaten without being heated up, but when you want to boil a pot of pasta and the power and gas are out, you will be glad you have your little stove.

YOUR PLAN

Write a list of equipment you need to buy in your Ready for Anything notebook. Be sure to add a due date for your shopping.

CHAPTER NINETEEN

PREP #16:
PREP YOUR PETS

My friend Tonya gave me the best compliment.

"I love how you think about Roger—you constantly think to yourself, and out loud, What would make Roger happy? and then you figure out a way to do it."

"Wow, Tonya," I replied, "I had no idea! That is the best compliment."

"Well," Tonya added, "to be fair, you also say that a lot about Jake."

Jake, you will remember, is our fifteen-year-old puggle.

I don't think I'm alone in this. I love my dog and will do whatever I can to make sure he is happy. I'd do the same for our cat, Ashley, too, but she doesn't currently require as much devoted attention as either Jake or Roger.

Here are some things to consider when stocking up for your pet in an emergency situation.

1. **Water.** As I mentioned before, I factored in additional water for our pets. Add in what they drink in a day (the

CDC recommends a gallon a day, but you know your pets, so stockpile accordingly.) That may be overkill, but if the power goes out in the summer, I know that water consumption will go up. I may also want to offer Jake a tub of water he can cool down in.

2. **Food.** I need to make sure that I have at least two weeks' worth of dry and canned food on hand. My dog, at his advanced age, is on a special diet that my vet has me cook in my kitchen and add vitamins to. (I've already declared that I will not be cooking for the humans and the dog on the same night.) I need to insure that I have food on hand that I can prepare without the aid of refrigeration.

3. **Treats.** Like you, your animal is going to want to have some comfort food on hand during trying times, especially when he may not have as much of your attention as normal. If anyone is stressed around Jake, he absorbs that stress like a kitchen sponge and hangs on to it. In a stressful situation, your pet will need some extra comforts, and having healthy treats on hand will be helpful to your pet and to you.

4. **Medications.** Make sure you have at least two weeks' worth of any medications on hand for your furry friend plus whatever you need to administer those meds. Since our dog is pretty old (and has grown pickier as he's gotten older), the only way he takes pills is if I stuff them into cheese pill pockets (and no, real cheese won't work). He also requires a shot every six weeks that the vet tech taught me to administer. I got over my fear of giving Jake shots and now know that I can take care of him no matter what our situation.

One of the resources I've recently picked up is the book *National Geographic Complete Guide to Pet Health, Behavior, and Happiness: The Veterinarian's Approach to At-Home Animal Care* by Gary Weitzman, DVM, MPH. I got this not only for emergency situations but also for day-to-day concerns for Jake and Ashley. The information helps me determine when to take them to the vet and when to wait out their health issues at home.

MAKE SURE YOUR PET IS ID'D

One of the most heartbreaking situations when it comes to natural disasters is to see the number of pets who are never reunited with their owners after being lost. One way to help prevent your pet from getting permanently separated from you during a disaster is to make sure your pet has proper identification.

Jake has been microchipped and wears a collar with his information on it. Ashley (an indoor cat) has also been microchipped, but she has been able to get out of any collar we've ever put on her. Letting her go without a collar makes us feel like bad parents, but it's the reality of our situation.

I found a dog years ago. He was hanging out in our local supermarket at the meat counter, waiting for someone to feed him. When I took Maximus (he was over 120 pounds) to the shelter, it turned out he was chipped, but the microchip was not registered. Please make sure that your pet's microchip is registered and that the information is updated if you move or change your contact information. But don't worry about Maximus. His mom ended up at the shelter the same time I was there with him. They were happily reunited, and she registered the microchip for Toast (his real name).

HAVE CRATES FOR EACH ANIMAL

If you end up going to a shelter in the midst of a natural disaster, some will accept pets only if they are crated. Make sure you have a crate that is big enough for your animal to stand up and lie down in.

ADD PETS TO YOUR EMERGENCY BINDER

In your emergency binder, have a section for your pets with vet contacts, updated immunization records (in case they need to be boarded, even for day care), prescriptions, and any other information you may need.

One of the other benefits of having this section completed is that you can copy it and have it available for anyone who is pet sitting for you.

PET BUG-OUT BAG

Each of your pets will need a bug-out bag with at least three days' worth of supplies. (I have a little duffel bag that holds all the supplies for both of our fur babies.)

The duffel should include the following items:

- food
- water
- food and water bowl—paper or plastic bowls are great when you're on the road. We have a collapsible water bowl for car trips with our animals, but we pack disposable bowls or wipes for cleaning bowls used for wet food.

- a three-day supply of medications packed and ready to go
- an extra leash for your dog and a new, small plastic pan and a bag of litter packed for your cat—cat litter can also help you get traction for your car in bad weather, but then you have to explain the lack of litter to your cat

HAVE A PLAN

Before a crisis hits, know where you will go if your house is uninhabitable for you and your pets. Red Cross shelters will not accept pets but may be able to point you to places that can accept your dog or cat.

We have already made arrangements with local friends (our zombie apocalypse teammates, Scott and Kelli) to bring our whole family (dog and cat included) to their home in the case of an emergency. We also have an out-of-town option, my mom, in case we need to leave the area altogether.

A great website, BringFido, at www.bringfido.com, tells you where you can find hotels, vacation rentals, campgrounds, and other establishments that allow dogs. Call ahead to make sure your cats are welcome as well.

Preparing for your pet as well as yourself can feel overwhelming, but let me give you an example of why it is so worth it. When we got the call that Roger's stepmom, Mary Jane, was killed in a car crash on Easter morning, we had less than twenty hours to pull everything together and get on a plane to get to the memorial, which was happening just two days later.

Since it was Easter, all the places we would normally get

Jake's prescription dog food were closed. But because we had a three-day bag ready, we had everything he needed to be boarded until my daughter could come be with him. I didn't have to spend precious time getting his overnight bag together, typing up instructions, and so on. Everything was ready to go, and it was one major check mark I was able to get because even our dog was ready for anything. In a time of grief and stress, I was set up so others could help us. And I had one less worry to contend with.

YOUR PLAN

Write out a detailed plan about how you will travel with your pets should you need to evacuate your home (include microchipping if you haven't already). Make a list of everything you need to buy for your bug-out bag and all the items you need to stock up on in case you're stranded at home without power and water for a couple of weeks.

Don't forget to add the deadline for completing these tasks.

TWENTY

PREP #17: PRACTICE YOUR PREP—HAVE A GRID-LIGHT DAY

One of the biggest mistakes we can make when trying to get ready for anything is trying to learn survival skills in the midst of a crisis.

Having all the "stuff" you need to get through an emergency is important. (Because in a major disaster, you can't rely on Amazon Prime to get you your stuff the same day.) But knowing how to use all that stuff before an emergency hits is crucial.

One of the surprisingly fun things Roger and I have done is practice "grid-light" days. I've mentioned this in previous chapters but want to address it fully here. A grid-light day is when we don't use something that we take for granted every day.

One month we did a day without electricity, and yes, that included internet. Another month we went for a day without water. Another month we did without our car for a day.

One day each month we tried to do what we needed to do without that one key "luxury." And it was not only educational but also entertaining.

I learned skills such as how to prepare freeze-dried food and how to change a propane tank. I learned to use headlamps to do things when the power was out and how to flush a toilet when there was no running water.

But can I tell you? It was also fun. I mean really fun. For instance, figuring out how to cook all our meals on a grill that, until that point, had only been used for steaks and veggies was a great challenge that really tested our creativity.

Partnering to make our house run brought Roger and I together in a new way. When our kids asked if we were doing anything the weekend we'd planned our day without electricity, we told them they were welcome to come over, but it would be a visit without power. We played board games, grilled our dinner, and lit candles as the evening turned into night. We laughed and talked, played Codenames and pinochle, and created a night to remember.

So my suggestion? Plan a grid-light day and see if you can practice some of the skills you will need when a real emergency takes place.

We have taken a whole day each month to live without these modern conveniences. But we don't just sit around, hunker down, and wait for the crack of dawn to hit in order to turn on the TV again. We use these times to make lists of supplies we still need to complete our preparedness. We, like you, are building our kits.

Or we will take an inventory of all of our food items and see if there is anything we are running low on, or look at the store flyers to see if there are any sales that we can take advantage of to stock up on items for our two-week supply.

As I mentioned in chapter 16 on prepping your kids, having a grid-light day is a wonderful way to introduce the concept of being prepared without provoking fear of disaster in your kids.

I also like to use a grid-light day as a way to prepare for the most common situation that we will face as a family—financial troubles. Having a day when you don't go out for food or entertainment and aren't using any electronic devices is a great way to grow closer as a family and have a fun project. Having to pull together as a team also ensures that you aren't the only one with information when a problem hits. All team members will have a role.

Every family has different priorities, of course. My friend Diane, whose son has special needs, told me that if her son could not have his iPad, "All hope would be lost." I suggested that they have a backup power source for just the iPad.

EVERYONE HAS A ROLE—
UNTIL THEY ARE NOT THERE

Part of doing a practice run is making sure that I can do everything that would normally be my husband's job, and vice versa. Having individual roles to play is great, but as I sit here at my laptop typing this, my only "teammates" who can help me out here at home are my geriatric dog and five-year-old cat who has never really been known for being a "team player."

Since my husband is at work and currently fourteen miles away from me (and judging from my commute time getting home after the '89 Loma Prieta earthquake, it could be a long time before we are reunited again), I need to know how to do all the things I would normally rely on him to do.

Even if you're the main person doing disaster preparedness and planning in your household, every family member needs to know what to do in a crisis.

DRILL, DRILL, DRILL

If we can take a lesson from the military, readiness depends on drilling often and continually tweaking our processes. As we work on getting ready for anything, our practice allows us to gradually become proficient at all the skills we'll need in a disaster. But unlike the military, we can make it a fun family activity that our kids will enjoy.

YOUR PLAN

Write some dates for grid-light days in your Ready for Anything notebook and put them on your calendar. Plan ahead for what you think you'll need on those days, like five-gallon buckets for "no water" day or briquettes for "no power" day.

Be sure to go back and add notes of lessons learned and other items you need to buy after your grid-light day.

TWENTY-ONE

21 WAYS TO BE READY FOR ANYTHING IN YOUR EVERYDAY LIFE

Being ready for anything isn't just a checklist of canned foods to buy in case of emergency. It's a complete mind-set change.

I spent most of my younger life catching up on life. Paying bills late, getting charged late fees at the library, paying for rush jobs on things at the last minute. As I got older and wiser, I started to get caught up on life—paying bills on time, returning books on time, thinking through my day to make sure I could complete all my work. But in the last couple of years, I've changed my thinking. It's not enough to be caught up. I want to be thinking ahead. I want to have time in my schedule so that if there is an emergency, my entire life is not a delicate game of dominoes ready to crash over because I've had one little bump in my day.

We have to go from "catch up" thinking in all areas of our lives to "I'm in control of some areas of my life, and in those areas, I will use planning and wisdom." Planning ahead will allow extra space, time, energy, and money in our lives. And all of those resources can become very valuable in a crisis.

Below are twenty-one ways you can up the preparedness factor in every area of your life:

1. GAS UP

Keep your gas tank at least half full all the time. If you have an emergency or need to get out of town quickly, the last thing you want to do is stop at a gas station.

I also keep a small amount of cash stashed in my car in a hard-to-get-to place. In other words, I would really have to be desperate to use it and not just dying for a Frappuccino.

2. STORE CAR KEYS IN THE SAME PLACE EVERY TIME

Keep your keys in the same place in your house every time you come home (preferably by the front door). That way, in an emergency, hunting for your car keys is one less thing you have to be worried about.

3. HAVE A SPECIFIED PLACE FOR YOUR PURSE OR BAG

Make sure you put your bag in the same place every time you get home so that it's easy to find in an emergency and just to be kind to your morning self, so you don't have to hunt for it before work or school drop-off.

4. CARRY CASH

You don't need to carry a lot of cash, but although many purchases are made with debit and credit cards these days, cash will still work most places and becomes even more valuable in an emergency.

5. KEEP YOUR LAPTOP CHARGED

Charge your laptop each night and carry a spare charger in your computer bag. I was grateful I had done this when I received a call in the middle of the night that my son was in the hospital with debilitating back pain (turned out it was appendicitis). I've been in enough ER waiting rooms to know to bring my laptop to work on while waiting for lab results, to see the doctor, and sometimes, for a loved one to come out of surgery. Plus, it's a great bonus to be able to look up insurance information on an actual laptop and not just on a tiny phone screen.

6. UPDATE YOUR PASSPORT

If you have family who live or are traveling out of the country, be sure your passport is up to date. When my first husband was involved in a head-on collision in England, I was able to get on the next plane to go be with him. Unfortunately, his parents, who hadn't done much international travel in their lives, had to wait two weeks for emergency passports to be able to go and visit him.

7. ASK YOURSELF "WHERE WILL THIS GO?"

Before you go to the store for anything, ask yourself, "Where will this go?" This includes canned tuna and new barbecue grills. Look at your space. If there isn't a hole where your purchase is going to go, create a space.

When I get home from fighting a crowd at a warehouse store, the last thing I want to do is reorganize so that I can find places for all my bargains. (I'm just grateful to escape with my life, much less eighty rolls of toilet paper!) I have now taken to creating those spaces before I leave so that when I get home, I just have to put away items, not rearrange my entire life.

8. SET UP YOUR COFFEE THE NIGHT BEFORE

No, this is not a lifesaving tip.

Hey wait . . . maybe it is. If you get hit with an urgent email first thing in the morning, or with a kid who was less than prepared (and now needs one more thing for a project), that cup of freshly brewed coffee might be a lifesaver (for you and your child).

For me, setting up my coffee the night before has had a couple of great outcomes. Not only do I save time in the morning (especially if I'm off to work outside the home early), but having coffee prepared is also my reward for waking up on time. It is much easier to get out of bed when the smell of fresh coffee promises me a wonderful cupful in just a few minutes.

Finally, I am not at all tempted to spend money at a coffee shop when the coffee is already made. As much as I love

Starbucks coffee as a treat, I'm not going to put on "outside clothes" to go get it if I have coffee in the pot.

9. DRESS FOR YOUR DAY

I used to get dressed in stages.

If my husband took the kids to school, I would shower and put on sweats since I wasn't leaving the house until two thirty. Then, around two o'clock, I would put on real clothes (so I wouldn't embarrass the children by looking like I just crawled out of bed) and go to pick them up.

I've now determined that it takes a lot less effort to get dressed once during the day. I was even forced to wear shoes in the house (thanks, plantar fasciitis!) and have found that I am much more willing to run to the store for a needed item, walk the dog, run out to the garage for an item, and stay on top of housework if I'm dressed and wearing shoes. Plus, if a situation does come up, I don't have to take time to get dressed; I can be out the door immediately.

10. ALWAYS HAVE A BACKUP

When it comes to household consumables, always have a backup.

I don't put trash bags on my warehouse shopping list when I'm running low on them. I put them on my list when I'm running low on the current box and have only one backup box. This works for all nonperishable parts of life—things such as the following:

- dry food (cereal, oatmeal, baking items)
- paper goods (towels, napkins, toilet paper, tissues)
- household goods (dish soap, garbage bags, laundry soap)
- personal hygiene items (soap, shampoo, razor blades, deodorant, toothpaste, etc.)
- over-the-counter meds

This little system has helped me out in a number of different situations:

- When I've been on a huge work deadline and going to the store seems about as impossible as getting *Hamilton* tickets in 2015
- When I've had the flu and leaving the house is the last thing I want to do
- When we've been low on money and needed to make it to our next paycheck
- When we've had friends in crisis who needed a little help to get to their next paycheck

11. FILE, DON'T PILE

Staying on top of your filing will help you be prepared in small ways every day. The warranty for your washer, the receipt for the light that didn't work, the proof that you paid your bill—you will only find these things if you actually file them. But only file what is completely necessary. Nobody ever needs to see your Target receipt from when you bought four Toblerone bars in one day. That can be our little secret.

12. DO A WALLET INVENTORY

Do yourself a favor now and take an inventory of everything in your wallet. Better yet, photocopy or scan everything in your wallet, and keep it in a place like Dropbox. If your wallet goes missing, you have all the debit card numbers and phone numbers, and any other info you need to cancel cards and get replacements quickly.

13. STASH A SMALL SEWING KIT

While attending a fancy event to honor the visiting president of the international missions board while I was a missionary in Japan, I wore my only dress-up outfit, a floral skirt and a sweater. When I got to the event, I was feeling pretty put together until the wife of the president sidled up to me and said, "I don't know if you're aware, but your hem has come undone." Well, of course I was mortified. That is, until she, the wife of the president of the international missions board, hustled me into a corner, got down on her hands and knees, and proceeded to whip a sewing kit out of her purse and stitch up my skirt like a professional seamstress.

MacGyver's got nothing on her.

Lesson learned—if you need to look put together, ninety-nine times out of one hundred, you won't need a sewing kit. But on that one-hundredth time, you will be so glad you have it.

I carry a small zippered pouch in my purse that holds these items:

- scissors
- needles

- easy threaders
- pins
- safety pins
- thimble
- measuring tape
- seam ripper
- 12 tiny spools of thread in various colors
- Hollywood tape (tape that helps you keep clothing in place—perfect for emergency hem repairs or a shirt that suddenly keeps falling open in wildly inappropriate ways)

And the good news? You can be a hero for someone else in a loose-button crisis.

14. GETTING OUT THE DOOR IS ALL ABOUT THE NIGHT BEFORE

- Prepare for your day at night. Make sure your purse, backpack, and laptop bag are ready to grab in the morning.
- Think through tomorrow's meals. This is a great time to do the following:
  PREP BREAKFAST: You can mix together eggs, milk, and seasonings for make-ahead scrambled eggs waiting in the fridge to pop on the stove top in the morning. Or find a great recipe for overnight oats. Even just putting the breakfast dishes on the table for your troops will save you time the next morning.

PACK LUNCH: I pack Roger's lunch at night when I am packing up the leftovers from dinner. If there are no leftovers, I just throw in the fixings for a hearty salad bowl (including some chicken for protein) along with some fruit and a treat. Nothing makes Roger feel more loved than having a packed lunch. (And if it were up to him, he would resort to fast food or Top Ramen every day. Packing his lunch saves us money and keeps me from being a widow due to sodium poisoning.)

PLAN DINNER: We all have the best of intentions when it comes to planning in the morning, but mornings are crazy, and my first impulse is to say, "I'll figure it out tonight." But then, as it's time to get dinner on the table, nothing is planned, nothing is defrosted, and I'll end up making a trip to the store for rotisserie chicken, a bag of salad, and a loaf of french bread. Again.

But the night before? Anything is possible. So write down what you want to cook, check on ingredients, pull meat out to defrost, and feel like a boss when it comes to dinner.

- Go to bed at a decent time. Everything goes better and I'm a nicer human when I get enough sleep.
- Set an alarm. If you're a serial snooze-button hitter, place your phone on the other side of your bed; this will require you to get up and get your day going.
- Open the blinds and curtains. Filling your room with daylight will help your body wake up.
- Eat that yummy breakfast you planned the night before.

- Do you know how long it takes you to get ready in the morning? If not, time yourself from the moment you get out of bed till you walk out the door. This will give you an idea of when you should wake up so you are not rushed. And if you don't want to wake up that early, it will also force you to figure out ways to create a better morning routine to get out the door on time if you're constantly falling behind.

- Stay consistent with your waking time each day. This will train your body to wake up naturally. Even on days when you don't have to get up early, do so. This will give you a wonderful break from your morning routine. You can spend time in the Word, sip your coffee, watch the news, or just enjoy the quietness of the house while the noisemakers (your family) sleep.

15. UP YOUR WATER GAME

As someone who has passed out twice because of dehydration, I know that it is easy to underestimate how much water you need each day. Planning breaks for water and getting a system going so that you are drinking water throughout the day is vital to staying healthy and alert. I have an app on my phone that is set to nag me at regular intervals to drink the water I need.

16. THINK THROUGH YOUR DAY

One of the best decisions I've made as an adult is, as I'm closing up from work each day, I take a peek at the next day's schedule to see if there is anything I can do to prepare for it. Do I need to prep a lunch (if I'm eating at home) or pack a lunch, or am I meeting someone for a business lunch? Am I going to the gym, or will walking the dog be my exercise in the morning? How dressed up do I need to be for the day? Do I need to set aside any time for deep thought, or is tomorrow just about getting things checked off the list? Thinking through your day will help you become a better planner and will help you know what will make tomorrow easier if only you do one thing to help today.

17. CREATE AN EVENING ROUTINE

Having a bedtime routine will help you sleep better at night and wake up to an already prepared wardrobe, coffee, and breakfast. Make a checklist of all the tasks you need to get ready for bed, and then follow it.

18. CREATE A MORNING ROUTINE

Save time by having a set routine you follow each morning. Set up your day for success by including tasks that will help you later in the day, like unloading the dishwasher.

19. START BATCH COOKING

Something I have done for more than twenty years now is batch cooking for my family. I pick ten different meals and then make three batches of each of them, freeze them, and then have a few meals a week that were premade.

For several years, I and five of my friends each made six family-size portions of three recipes, packaged them up, and froze them; and then, on an early Saturday morning, we would gather in a warehouse store parking lot and swap all those meals. Each of us would go home with eighteen different meals. We would use three a week, and then, six weeks later, we would do it all again. It was amazing.

And now my kids, who are all adults, want to do batch cooking because they realize how much time, money, and energy it saves at the end of a long day of work.

If you don't want to start out at the pro level of eighteen meals in a day, start by doubling any recipe that can be frozen and put those meals away for a busy day when you know you won't have time to make something from scratch.

20. SPEND TIME ORGANIZING, EVERY DAY

I spend fifteen minutes decluttering and organizing every day. I've found that the more I stay on top of it, the easier it becomes and the more I actually enjoy it. Every day I spend those fifteen minutes in a different room, and it makes all the difference when it comes to staying on top of where things are and being prepared. At first you may find this routine over-whelming, but I promise that the more that you stay on top of your clutter, the easier being organized will become.

21. TRADE KEYS

Yesterday evening I received the call every parent gets at one point in his or her life: "Um . . . Mom . . . I locked my keys in my car. Can you bring me my spares?" This was my daughter who works in another city, but that's what a mom does for the kid she loves.

But the ready for anything part of this story? As soon as Kimberly drove her new car off the lot, she drove straight to our house and gave me her spare key. I've had that key for four years, and it had never been touched until last night. In fact, I had forgotten about it to the point that it didn't even occur to me to talk about having a key at someone else's house until she called last night. (I felt bad for her, but I loved that I had another point to put in my book. There are no problems in life, just additional things to write about.)

Make sure you have a spare key with someone you trust. It could be a neighbor, a friend, or a family member.

TWENTY-TWO

READY FOR ANYTHING *AND* A CLEAN HOUSE

If you've read any of my other books, chances are it was *Clutter Free*—an entire book about decluttering your home. Once that book was published, I realized that clutter and organization were the topics I was most interested in writing, speaking, and teaching about. So how does being ready for anything fit into that?

Getting rid of clutter is all about cleaning up your past. Organization is taking care of yourself in the present. And being ready for anything means taking care of your future self. All three are important. All three are taking care of you.

One of the things I would encourage you to do as you are preparing yourself for the future is, at the same time, to take care of your past and your present by cleaning out clutter and getting organized. Does that seem overwhelming? I can hear it now. "Kathi, I can't make progress on decluttering and organizing in my regular life, and now you want me to do those things *and* prepare for an emergency. I am already overwhelmed."

I get it. I really do. But here is the secret: before, you were decluttering because you were just tired of all the extra stuff in your house and you wanted it gone. But now, because you are getting ready for anything, you have a criteria for getting rid of stuff. If you have determined that you need four shelves in your basement for all your preparedness supplies but you haven't seen the top of a shelf since 2006, you now have a concrete goal for getting rid of stuff.

And everything you've ever saved because you wonder if, in an emergency, you might need it? You can now think about it in the light of a crisis. Ask yourself, "In a crisis, will I be glad that I saved this Care Bears sleeping bag from my childhood just in case?" No. You have real criteria to decide whether something will actually be useful or not. The Bears? They have to go.

Clutter is the big lie of preparedness. Clutter tells you that you already have everything you need; you just may not be able to find it right now. "That's okay," Clutter says. "You will find it if you really need it."

Here's the problem with that: in a crisis you don't have the time or mental capacity to find the pack of batteries you know you have "somewhere."

Clutter tells you that you have plenty of food for an emergency, when in reality you have a ton of canned fruits and salmon but nothing to eat them with. Clutter tells you that you were smart enough to stock up when canned soup went on sale at the grocery store, until you realize that all that soup expired in 2013.

I've been seriously dealing with my clutter and organization for about ten years now. My dad would have been classified as a hoarder by some, so this has been a lifelong struggle. But I took both my decluttering and organization to a new level when I started getting ready for anything.

1. I deeply decluttered. It is easy to keep clutter when it's neatly organized and in labeled boxes. Oh, I could justify keeping it (in case I need it someday), but when it came down to whether I wanted to keep those things or keep putting off being prepared for an emergency because I didn't have room to store "all that stuff," I realized I was using clutter as an excuse not to think through a crisis.

2. I got out of "just in case" thinking and got into "ready for anything" thinking. "Just in case" thinking is when you say, "I'm going to hold on to this stuff just in case I need it someday." "Ready for anything" thinking says, "I have a list here of the things I need to take care of myself, my family, and my neighbor when a crisis happens."

   "Just in case" thinking is based on fear. "Ready for anything" thinking is based on compassion and wisdom.

   Fear is no longer the ruling force in what I allow to stay in my home. Instead of thinking vaguely, *But what if I need it someday?* I now think, *What do I need in a crisis to take care of myself and the people around me?*

3. I did an inventory (with expiration dates). Being prepared means that your stuff actually works and will serve you when the time comes. That means you've tested the flashlights, you have propane for the grill, and your food is something you'll actually eat.

4. I kept things current.

5. Everything has a purpose.

6. With organization, I actually know where to find things. I love that I know where things are and can find them quickly. I know how many cans of soup I have, when that soup is expiring, and what I need to help me and those I love be safe and comfortable.

7. I stay on top of things. Traditional prepping says you buy ten years of supplies and forget about them until disaster hits. But the ready for anything plan says that you are using your food, practicing your skills, and staying on top of your systems. If you spend fifteen minutes every day decluttering, organizing, and preparing, that will be so much easier than trying to do a massive overhaul. All three of these areas become a part of your everyday life, and that makes every single area of your life that much better.

DECLUTTER: THE DAILY METHOD

If you don't have an overwhelming amount of clutter, I suggest you take fifteen minutes a day and get rid of anything you don't need or want. I use the three boxes, two bags system.

The Three Boxes, Two Bags System

You will use the three boxes, two bags system in almost every room in your house, so gather up everything you'll need right now.

Set up three cardboard boxes, a garbage bag, and a recycle bag, and a timer (you can use the one on your cell phone or your oven).

Mark one cardboard box "Other Rooms," one "Put Back," and one "Give Away."

Set fifteen minutes on your timer and pick a spot to clean out (an area no larger than what you can sort through in fifteen minutes). Go through the area and use the three boxes to sort the contents.

Other Rooms Box

Anything that doesn't belong in the area you're cleaning goes into the "Other Rooms" box. This includes toys in the kitchen, dog brushes in the living room, report cards in the bathroom, or dishes in the bedroom.

Put Back Box

This "Put Back" box is the box where you put things that belong in the area you're cleaning, but they need to be put back in the right place. If you're straightening up your bedroom, examples of items that you would place in this box are clean clothes on the floor, shoes under your bed, or scarves hanging over a bedroom chair. Once you have your bedroom in order, you just put those items back where they belong.

Give Away Box

Clothes your kids have outgrown? Check. Videos your family will never watch again? Check. There is great freedom in giving stuff away. Here is a great set of criteria for keeping or giving away an item:

- Is it something you or a family member is currently using or wearing?
- Is it something that makes you or a family member happy when they see it?

- Is it something you or a family member will definitely use in the year?

If you can answer yes to one or more of those questions, find a home for the item. If not, away it goes.

And a friendly reminder: don't donate garbage. It costs charities time and money to get rid of stuff that you don't want. Don't be that person. Donate only those things that are in decent condition and are worthy of reselling.

Garbage Bag

Anything that you don't want and that isn't worthy of being donated or can't be recycled goes in here.

Recycle Bag

Recycling regulations vary from city to city, so check with your local municipality or disposal service if you have any question about what should be recycled and what shouldn't.

Once you've cleaned out your chosen area, take the "Other Rooms" box and go around the house putting away all the stuff in that box. Take the "Give Away" box to where you gather stuff to donate, or take it directly to your car to be donated the next time you run errands. Now, since your area is clean and organized, put anything in the "Put Back" box into the spot it's supposed to go.

If this process feels overwhelming to you, consider having a supportive friend or someone you hire go through these steps with you. There's a lot of freedom in a fresh start.

THE DUMPSTER METHOD

If you honestly have years and years' worth of clutter—or, let's face it, garbage—you may need to use the dumpster method.

The dumpster method only works if a few factors are in play:

1. You can afford to get a dumpster.

   Dumpster rentals can vary wildly depending on size, service, and state. I've often seen the "$99 Dumpster Rentals!" but what the ad doesn't tell you is that price is just for renting the dumpster, not for delivery or dumping the junk. So do your research and find out how much it will actually cost.

2. You have a time limit.

   If you feel like you have all the time in the world, you will not use your dumpster efficiently. Plan on having your dumpster delivered a week from now, and start creating a pile of everything you want to dump so you can have a huge feeling of satisfaction as soon as the dumpster arrives at your home. (Also create a pile of everything in good shape that you want to donate, and schedule a charity pickup for the same day the dumpster is coming.)

   Having so much stuff out of your living and storage space will leave you feeling great. You will want to keep going and get rid of as much stuff as possible.

3. You have someone who can help you.

   Don't declutter alone. Clutter is indecision, and when you are stuck in indecision, you need someone who doesn't have emotional or financial attachment to stuff to help you make clearheaded decisions.

I ask myself (or a friend who is trying to declutter) these three guiding questions:

1. "Do I love it?" If you love it, you get to keep it. But if you say that you "love" it, and it's stuffed in a box in your garage that you haven't opened in four years, I question your love. If you truly love it, have it in your house where you can love it every single day.

2. "Do I use it?" If you use it, you get to keep it. Not, "Oh, I used that pizza pan six years ago when I thought I was a chef, but it turns out I just love watching *America's Test Kitchen* and ordering pizza." If you are not currently using it, and don't have plans to use it in the near future, it is clutter.

3. "Would I buy it again?" This is the most important question for those of us who are getting ready for anything. Do I love my emergency kit? Not really. Do I use it? No—thank goodness it hasn't come to that. "Would I buy it again?" Yes, if I lost the kit somehow, I would buy it again because I know it's important to have on hand.

DECLARE A SPACE

Now that you've cleared out some clutter (You're welcome!), it's time to get yourself organized and start making some meaning out of all this preparedness madness.

Finding nooks and crannies to stash all your preparedness materials is easy. But when a crisis hits, you won't want to have to go looking for anything. So declare a corner, a shelf, a cabinet, or a closet ready for anything sacred space. You may have to declare a couple of spaces. (It probably doesn't make sense to keep your canned corn and your sleeping bags on the same shelf.) Define those areas, and don't let anything else (especially clutter) sneak into them.

LABEL EVERYTHING

I like to organize the same way a kindergarten teacher would—with labels and signs so everyone knows where everything belongs. This also keeps people (kids, spouses, and ourselves) from shoving things into slots where they don't belong. And my favorite part about this? If the space is labeled, you know when something is missing.

TAKE A PICTURE

When you get everything just the way that you want it (or close enough), take a picture and hang that picture in the space. That way you will know when something is out of place and be able to correct the situation quickly.

While some people imagine that prepping means having to build additional rooms for all the extra stuff they will need to buy, you and I know better. It's not about having more stuff. It's about having the right stuff.

TWENTY-THREE

READY FOR ANYTHING AND LOVING YOUR NEIGHBOR

When the email message said the committee would be meeting at the elementary school, I wondered how I would know which room we would be meeting in.

I shouldn't have worried. Turns out our local elementary school is literally a one-room schoolhouse for students kindergarten through eighth grade.

Welcome to mountain living.

It was my first time connecting with members of our newly adopted community, and I was excited to be a part of the newly formed Omo Ranch Fire Safety Council Fund-Raising Committee.

Our writer's retreat center is in the middle of the Eldorado Forest of Northern California, just a couple of hours away from Paradise, California, where the Camp Fire decimated 95 percent of the town. As you can imagine, fire safety is the number one concern in our community.

One of our neighbors, Paul, has donated a fire truck to our community and is a volunteer firefighter. The criteria to serve in this role? He passed a test running up a mountain in full gear, carrying a fire hose in the blazing heat.

My contribution? Selling raffle tickets at the hot dog cook-off and silent auction fund-raiser.

Hey, we all have our special set of skills.

If you've spent a lot of time on prepper websites, you may have noticed a strong theme: "Take care of you and your family, but be prepared to defend yourself against your neighbor." But after talking with dozens of people who survived such tragedies as the Houston flood, the Bay Area earthquake, and the Paradise fires, I know one thing for certain: the main reason many people survived (and later thrived) was because of neighbors and strangers helping each other out.

And let's be clear as crystal—there is nothing in God's Word that supports an "every man for himself" approach to life. In fact, Scripture points over and over again to the fact that our best lives are achieved when we are serving and doing life with others. Here are a few examples:

No one should seek their own good, but the good of others. (1 Corinthians 10:24)

For the entire law is fulfilled in keeping this one command: "Love your neighbor as yourself." (Galatians 5:14)

Carry each other's burdens, and in this way you will fulfill the law of Christ. (Galatians 6:2)

Keep on loving one another as brothers and sisters.
Do not forget to show hospitality to strangers, for by
so doing some people have shown hospitality to angels
without knowing it. (Hebrews 13:1–2)

It's easy to get protective when it comes to prepping. We think about how much food our family will need and how much money it will take to survive. But in all the plans I've made to be better prepared, I've needed to keep the most important question at the front of my mind. How do I serve my neighbor well? Because when I take my eyes off of me, and my family's needs, and start to look at the people around me, I can work not only to take care of my household but the households around us. I can truly be the hands and feet of Jesus to those whom God has put in my path.

So how do you go from being self-focused to community focused while still making sure your needs are being covered?

GET INVOLVED IN YOUR COMMUNITY SO YOU CAN LEARN HOW YOU AND YOUR CHURCH CAN MEET THEIR NEEDS

Many of us who have a heart for our communities reach out by starting at our church and then moving from the church to outreach in the community. That can be an amazing way to serve.

Last month I did a presentation about my book *Clutter Free* at the library I grew up going to, Santa Clara Public Library. It was a wonderful event, and I love giving back to my community in this way. I had several people come up to me after the presentation to ask questions and get more resources. One of those women, I'll call her Claire, wanted to talk to me privately. She had become disabled, and her clutter had grown out of control. She didn't know where to begin. "Do you know of any organizations that help the elderly or disabled in our community?" she asked.

I told her I would research her question and get back to her with what I could find. I felt a little helpless. I knew there were businesses that helped, but I also knew they charged thousands of dollars. When I mentioned it to Roger, he said, "Hey, I think there are some community groups at church that have helped people in those situations before. Why not talk to Susan?"

Susan is the director of our local compassion team at Church on the Hill in San Jose. When I emailed her asking if she knew of any resources, she replied that she would get a couple of crews to the woman's house within two weeks.

I knew that with a book deadline, two out-of-state speaking engagements, and a move, there was no way I was going to be able to participate, but I asked if I could pay for the trash removal, garbage bags, or cleaning supplies.

Susan let me know they had all the man (and woman) power they needed to get the job done, and because of a generous church member, they even had the disposal of all the "stuff" covered. All I needed to do was connect Susan and Claire and be grateful for the church I am a part of.

Belonging to a church that reaches out to the community for crises big and small sets your heart to thinking beyond yourself. That's part of why we need to make sure our needs are met (through being 3-2-3 ready): once we have passed our own crisis, we can move on and help our neighbor. It's much harder to help feed others when we don't have provisions of our own. Be prepared to take care of your own needs so you can then move on to take care of the needs around you.

KNOW YOUR NEIGHBORS

In our first winter at the mountain house, we were busy trying to get ready for our next writers retreat by plowing our quarter-mile driveway and restoring our power and water after a huge storm.

We invited two guys who were looking for day work to help us with snow removal. When we told them of the road conditions, and the need for four-wheel drive, their response? "Great—we'll be fine." They did not have a four-wheel drive, but in their minds thought they could make it anyway.

As you can imagine, that ended up with them being hopelessly stuck on our mountain.

But, gratefully, we'd already met a few neighbors. One had a tow truck, the others had manpower. Between them, Roger, and our two helpers, they were able to get the guys unstuck and on their way home.

Sometimes you are the one helping your neighbor. And sometimes you are the one requiring a tow truck.

I was grateful we'd had an opportunity to connect with the people on the mountain before the snowstorm of the decade rendered us unable to get off the mountain.

We have similar relationships with our neighbors at our home in San Jose. We know each other's names and kids, take each other's dogs on walks if we're late at work, and have each other's keys in case someone gets locked out of their homes.

But what if you don't know your neighbors? How do you start to get connected as a community?

1. Offer Help

Roger is the fix-it man of the twenty-first century. He has helped our neighbors get their printers up and running, installed electronic doorbells, and troubleshot phone systems. I've taken the neighbor's garbage out when they are on vacation, dropped neighbors off at the airport, and brought in packages from their front door after leaving a note that I have their goods at my house. (Porch pirates are a huge issue in our neighborhood.) Offering small, simple ways of helping strengthens relationships and makes it easier to ask for—and offer—help for bigger situations and emergencies.

2. Offer Food

Roger and I put on a huge conference every year at our church, which we pay for personally. One of the nights we order an Italian feast from a local restaurant. Because we're never sure who will eat what, we always have a lot of leftovers. Along with offering the church's youth group all the leftover desserts (which has made us wildly popular with the young people at church), we bring containers to church to take the leftovers back to our neighborhood. We ring doorbells and hand out platters of rigatoni and chicken piccata.

One of our next-door neighbors has three small kids. When we had two dozen beautiful Ruby Red apples left over from an event, they gratefully received those apples. It was a simple way of getting to connect with them again in a low-stakes way: the apples were free to us, so they felt no obligation or need to return the favor.

3. Offer Stuff

We finally bought a garden "chipper" (a contraption that you feed branches into that turns them into mulch), not because of our garden, but for our next-door neighbors.

Next to our town house is a rental unit with a giant bougainvillea bush. A bush wouldn't seem like a big deal, but living in a town house, we have a tiny patio, and this bougainvillea was an out-of-control monster taking over our backyard. It grew really fast, had thorny branches, and dropped leaves all over the place. And for the first fifteen years Roger lived there, he would have to trim that bush back from being on our property, which would take an hour or two, depending on how out of control it had become. The landlord never returned our calls to deal with it, so to be good neighbors to the parade of renters going through that house, Roger just quietly took care of the bush on our side.

After fifteen years, he finally decided to buy the chipper to make the job easier. Those branches grew long and had to be cut down before going into our green waste cart.

And then, our most recent neighbor, Rob, moved in. I came out one day, and there was Rob trimming our side of the bougainvillea bush. Glory be!

I called over to Rob, "Wow, thank you for taking care of our side!"

Rob's reply? "Of course! I want to be a good neighbor!"

Then, I knew how we could all help each other. "Hey, Rob, would you like to use our chipper?"

I think I may have seen tears in his eyes. "Yes, I would love to use your chipper!" (It really is a terrible job.)

By sharing our stuff, we've gone a little deeper in our

neighborliness. I feel that Rob's family is free to ask for the next thing they need, and if we have a need, we would be able to ask them.

Oh, and Rob has stopped asking to use the chipper—because he got permission from his landlord to rip that bougainvillea out by its roots. Praise be!

I think about the church in Acts, and how they shared what they had: "All the believers were one in heart and mind. No one claimed that any of their possessions was their own, but they shared everything they had" (Acts 4:32). While we haven't gotten to that level with our neighbors, sharing what we have in the good times builds a bond that can be called on during times of challenge.

4. Offer Friendship

When we are barbecuing, we either throw on an extra burger for our neighbor Diane, who lives alone, or invite her over to join us for dinner. She loves barbecue but rarely fires up her grill.

It has taken some time, but we now know most of the neighbors around us. We ask after their kids and dogs, we cheer on their grandkids when they are learning to ride bikes. Just by being friendly, we can help foster a place of acceptance and love in our tiny community.

During nice weather we carry out a couple of camping chairs and sit in the middle of our grass cul-de-sac with our puggle Jake on his leash and just talk. As neighbors come by with their kids and dogs, they will stop and talk and sometimes sit for a while. This is the number one way we've gotten to know our neighbors.

5. Join a Cyber Community

In the city, we are part of the Nextdoor app. In the mountains, we are part of a Facebook page dedicated to our community. Both of these tools have helped us get to know our communities and helped when there has been a crisis.

Near our San Jose home, which normally has a pretty low crime rate, recently there was a tragic murder that has had political implications. We as a community were able to stay connected, to mourn together, care for each other, and organize because of the Nextdoor app.

And in the mountains, because of the Facebook page, we can know who is experiencing a power outage, discover the most up-to-date information from our power company, help out snowbound neighbors, and know what roads are closed either from snowpack or from a cow that refuses to budge.

The only warning I have about cyber communities is that you will need to be willing to filter out what some of the cranks and naysayers are whining about. Even though these are real people who live in your community, the anonymity of the internet makes people feel as if they can say whatever they want without any consequences. Don't use the space for moral debates. Use it to help find your neighbor's lost dog or to prepare for a storm.

NEXT-LEVEL NEIGHBORLINESS

Next-level neighborliness is when you actively consider your neighbors in your preparedness.

When Roger and I started our stockpile of food and water, we took into consideration our kids who live locally (all of whom live in tiny apartments and don't have a lot of space for stockpiling), and our next-door neighbor. We know that if there were ever an emergency, we would want to make sure she was taken care of, so we made sure she is part of our plan.

Next-level neighborliness can also be things like getting together with your neighbors to have a neighborhood plan in case of emergency. One of my friends lives in a community where, after a disaster, everyone is instructed to hang a piece of fabric outside their door to indicate that they are okay. If a neighbor sees that someone does not have that piece of fabric hanging outside their door, they will check on them right away.

It is my goal, slowly but surely, to make sure that we get to next-level neighborliness in both our neighborhoods.

Connecting with your neighbors before an emergency is one of the smartest things you can do. There is a world of difference between asking strangers for help and asking friends (or at least people you are friendly with) for help. You want your neighbors to see you as a first choice for help during a disaster, not the last resort.

READY FOR REAL

Friend, you've hung with me until the end. And for that, I thank you.

I know that prepping is a topic that can be uncomfortable, overwhelming, and even a little scary. You've hung in there until the end of the book, so that tells me a little something about you.

You are ready. Yes, it will take a lot of small steps and it will take time, but you are ready to start getting ready, and that is a beautiful place to be.

You care. You care about your people, and you want to love your neighbor well—enough so that you are willing to say, in a disaster, "I want to be a helper, not the person who needs a helper." When we have more people like you in our communities, we will be better together.

As we move forward, let me ask you to do a couple of things:

1. Join me over at KathiLipp.com/rfa. We have more resources, downloads for your binder, and more ways to help you become even more prepared.
2. Ask a friend to prep with you. Being part of a community (even if it's just a community of two) will help you stay focused and moving forward in your efforts to be ready for anything.

You are making my dream come true, friend—my dream of people all over the world who are ready to take care of not only themselves in the event of overwhelming circumstances but their neighbor as well. My dream of all of us being Jesus's hands and feet when the world needs us most. May you indeed be ready for anything, prepared for the unexpected, and unafraid of the future.